TEA
The Mythical Beginnings

Kevin B DiBacco

ISBN: 978-93-67005-83-5
eISBN: 978-93-67006-42-9

©Author

Cover design © 2024 Yellow Dog Digital Studios.
All rights reserved
Publisher: Pharos Books (P) Ltd.
Plot No.-63, 1st Floor, Main Mother Dairy Road
Pandav Nagar, East Delhi-110092
Phone: 011-40395855, +4049916623
WhatsApp: +91 8368220032
E-mail: sales@pharosbooks.in
Website: www.pharosbooks.in
First Edition: 2024

TEA: THE MYTHICAL BEGINNINGS
By Kevin B DiBacco

CONTENTS

DISCLAIMER

No part of this publication may be reproduced in any form or by any means, including printing, scanning, photocopying, or otherwise, without the prior written permission of the copyright holder. The author has tried to present information that is as correct and concrete as possible. The author is not a medical doctor and does not write in any medical capacity. All medical decisions should be made under the guidance and care of your primary physician. The author will not be held liable for any injury or loss that is incurred to the reader through the application of the information here contained in this book. The author points out that the medical field is fast evolving with newer studies being done continuously, therefore the information in this book is only a researched collaboration of accurate information at the time of writing. With the ever-changing nature of the subjects included, the author hopes that the reader will be able to appreciate the content that has been covered in this book. While all attempts have been made to verify each piece of information provided in this publication, the author assumes no responsibility for any error, omission, or contrary interpretation of the subject present in this book. Please note that any help or advice given hereof is not a substitution for licensed medical advice. The reader accepts responsibility in the use of any information and takes advice given in this book at their own risk. If the reader is under medication supervision or has had complications with health-related risks, consult your primary care physician as soon as possible before taking any advice given in this book.

"The information and advice contained in this book are based upon the research and the personal and professional experiences of the author. They are not intended as a substitute for consulting with a healthcare professional. The publisher and author are not responsible for any adverse effects or consequences resulting from the use of any of the suggestions, preparations, or procedures discussed in this book. All matters pertaining to your physical health should be supervised by a healthcare professional."

ABOUT THE AUTHOR

Kevin understands adversity and the temptation to quit better than most. His life has been a testament to the power of perseverance despite severe hardship. Now, he shares his story and tools to inspire others to get off the mat when knocked down by life.

Kevin's health struggles began early, needing major surgery at just 16 years old. In his 20s and 30s, he endured 6 knee operations, 2 back surgeries, including spinal fusion, 2 hip replacements, and treatment for an aggressive brain tumor. Enduring over 10 major medical procedures would be enough to make anyone want to give up. Even as he was writing this, Kevin was struck by Covid-19. As if that wasn't another setback, Kevin developed Pneumonia and spent the spring of 2022 and the summer of 2023 having to get daily nebulizer treatments. Once again, his theories were put to the test. Once again, they worked!

But Kevin refused to see himself as a victim of circumstance. Through each diagnosis and rehabilitation, he consciously worked to reframe adversity as an opportunity for growth. Instead of sadly ruminating on limitations, he focused positively on each small win: standing, walking, and climbing stairs: during recovery. He visualized himself healed and happy against all odds.

Kevin leaned on his deep faith and the support of loved ones during the darkest times. When fear or hopelessness crept in, he prayed for the strength to take the next step forward. He turned to uplifting books and sayings for encouragement. Slowly but surely, he reclaimed his active lifestyle step by step.

Through his journey, Kevin realized firsthand the power of mindset to figure out one's life experience. He discovered that he could transform his outer reality by controlling his inner world: his thoughts, beliefs, and visualizations. Now, he hopes to share these lessons with others facing major life challenges.

Kevin's book recounts his medical battles, along with the techniques he used to stay grounded in positivity. He provides exercises to overcome negative self-talk, face fears, and visualize desired outcomes. Kevin believes we can all learn to reframe difficulties as growth opportunities. Wherever we feel like quitting, he urges us to proclaim, "I will keep going!"

Kevin's dramatic story provides living proof that, regardless of what knocks us down, we can choose to get back up. We all have access to inner reserves of strength to endure the unendurable. Kevin hopes his book will inspire others to fight major life battles to find their power to keep progressing. By committing to personal growth, we can overcome any obstacle, including those within our minds.

Chapter 1

Introduction to Tea

Tea has captivated the world for millennia, its history rich and deeply intertwined with the cultures that have embraced it. Originating in ancient China, tea's discovery is steeped in legend. It is said that in 2737 BC, the legendary Emperor Shen Nong, known as the "Divine Farmer," was sitting beneath a Camellia sinensis plant while his servant boiled drinking water over an open fire. As the wind rustled the branches, a few leaves were carried aloft and gently fell into the emperor's simmering water, infusing it with a delightful aroma and enticing golden hue. Intrigued, Shen Nong took a sip and was instantly captivated by the invigorating and refreshing taste. Thus, tea was born, ushering in a new era of culinary and cultural exploration.

From these mythical beginnings, tea rapidly spread throughout China, becoming an integral part of daily life, social customs, and spiritual rituals. The Chinese mastered the cultivation and production of tea, developing various processing methods that gave rise to the diverse array of tea varieties we know today. Green tea, black tea, oolong tea, white tea, and puerh tea each boast their own unique characteristics, flavors, and potential health benefits.

As trade routes expanded and cultures intermingled, tea's popularity transcended borders, captivating nations across the globe. In India, the tea industry flourished under British colonial rule, with plantations sprouting up in regions like Assam and Darjeeling. India quickly became one of the world's largest tea producers, developing its own distinct tea culture and traditions, such as the quintessential masala chai.

Japan, too, embraced tea wholeheartedly, elevating it to an art form with the revered Japanese tea ceremony, or "chanoyu." This ritual, steeped in Zen Buddhist principles, celebrates the preparation and consumption of matcha, a finely ground powdered green tea. The tea ceremony is a choreographed sequence of precise movements and gestures, designed to foster harmony, respect, purity, and tranquility.

Beyond its cultural significance, tea has also been revered for its potential health benefits throughout history. Traditional Chinese medicine has long harnessed the healing properties of various tea varieties, utilizing them to treat a range of ailments and promote overall well-being. Green tea, in particular, has been the subject of numerous scientific studies, with researchers exploring its high concentration of polyphenols, specifically catechins like epigallocatechin gallate (EGCG).

These potent antioxidants have been linked to a multitude of health benefits, including:

1. **Improved heart health:** Green tea may help lower cholesterol levels, reduce blood pressure, and improve blood flow, thereby decreasing the risk of cardiovascular disease.

2. **Cancer prevention:** The antioxidants in green tea

  TEA: *The Mythical Beginnings*

have been shown to inhibit the growth and spread of certain types of cancer cells, including breast, prostate, and lung cancer.

3. **Weight management:** Green tea may boost metabolism and increase fat burning, aiding in weight loss efforts when combined with a balanced diet and regular exercise.

4. **Diabetes management:** Some studies suggest that the compounds in green tea may improve insulin sensitivity and help regulate blood sugar levels.

5. **Brain function:** The combination of caffeine and L-theanine, an amino acid found in green tea, has been shown to improve focus, alertness, and cognitive performance.

But green tea isn't the only variety with potential health benefits. Black tea, which undergoes a process of oxidation that alters its chemical composition, has also been studied for its potential effects on health. Research has suggested that black tea may:

1. **Improve gut health:** The polyphenols in black tea may promote the growth of beneficial gut bacteria, supporting digestion and overall gut health.

2. **Reduce risk of stroke:** Regular consumption of black tea has been associated with a lower risk of ischemic stroke, possibly due to its ability to improve blood vessel function.

3. **Support bone health:** Compounds in black tea may help increase bone mineral density and reduce the risk of osteoporosis.

4. **Boost immune function:** The antioxidants in black tea may help strengthen the immune system and reduce the risk of certain infections.

Even herbal teas, which are technically not derived from the Camellia sinensis plant, offer their own unique benefits. Chamomile tea, for instance, has been used for centuries as a natural remedy for promoting relaxation and aiding sleep. Its compounds, such as apigenin, have been shown to have mild sedative and anti-anxiety effects.

Peppermint tea, on the other hand, is renowned for its ability to soothe digestive issues like bloating, gas, and indigestion. The menthol in peppermint tea has a calming effect on the digestive tract and can also help alleviate nausea and vomiting.

As tea's popularity has soared globally, researchers have delved deeper into understanding its chemical composition and the mechanisms behind its potential health effects. One area of particular interest is the role of epigallocatechin gallate (EGCG), the most abundant and potent catechin found in green tea.

EGCG has been extensively studied for its antioxidant properties and its ability to neutralize free radicals, which are unstable molecules that can damage cells and contribute to the development of chronic diseases. Additionally, EGCG has been found to have anti-inflammatory effects, potentially reducing the risk of conditions like rheumatoid arthritis, inflammatory bowel disease, and certain types of cancer.

Interestingly, the benefits of EGCG may extend beyond its antioxidant and anti-inflammatory properties. Some research suggests that EGCG may also have neuroprotective effects, potentially reducing the risk of neurodegenerative diseases like

TEA: *The Mythical Beginnings*

Alzheimer's and Parkinson's. It may also play a role in regulating glucose metabolism, making it a potential therapeutic target for diabetes management.

While the research on tea's health benefits is promising, it's important to note that most studies have been conducted in controlled laboratory settings or with animal models. More extensive human clinical trials are needed to fully understand the extent of tea's potential health benefits and to determine safe and effective dosages.

Despite the ongoing research, one thing is clear: tea has deeply permeated cultures around the world, transcending its role as a mere beverage and becoming a symbol of hospitality, relaxation, and tradition.

In Morocco, the pouring of Maghrebi mint tea is an art form, with tea servers skillfully pouring the fragrant brew from great heights, creating a frothy head and a mesmerizing spectacle. The ritual of sharing mint tea is deeply ingrained in Moroccan culture, serving as a symbol of hospitality and a means of fostering connections between family and friends.

In Argentina and Uruguay, yerba mate, a type of herbal tea made from the dried leaves of the Ilex paraguariensis plant, is more than just a beverage – it's a way of life. The mate gourd, filled with the loose-leaf blend and sipped through a metal straw (bombilla), is passed around in a communal ritual that strengthens social bonds and promotes a sense of shared identity.

Even in the bustling streets of London, tea remains an integral part of daily life. The iconic afternoon tea tradition, with its tiered stands of dainty sandwiches, scones, and pastries, is a beloved ritual that harkens back to the 19th century, when Anna, the 7th Duchess of Bedford, is credited with popularizing the practice of taking tea and light refreshments in the late afternoon.

As the world continues to evolve, tea's enduring appeal and cultural significance show no signs of waning. From the modern-day tea houses of Tokyo to the chai wallahs (tea vendors) lining the streets of India, tea remains a constant thread woven through the tapestry of human experience, connecting us to our past while offering a comforting respite in the present.

Chapter 2

The History of Tea

Tea, that modest yet captivating brew, has woven itself into the fabric of human civilization for millennia, transcending its role as a mere beverage and emerging as a cultural touchstone, a symbol of tradition, and a potent elixir revered for its healing properties. Its journey through time is a tapestry of myth, ritual, and scientific exploration, spanning vast empires and diverse cultures, each leaving an indelible mark on the evolution of this beloved libation.

Ancient Origins: The Birth of Tea in China

The origins of tea are cloaked in the mists of legend and folklore, but most accounts trace its discovery to ancient China, where the reverence for this aromatic infusion took root. According to one of the most enduring tales, tea was first discovered by the mythical Emperor Shen Nong, renowned as the "Divine Farmer" and the father of Chinese agriculture.

In the year 2737 BCE, as the emperor sat beneath the shade of a Camellia sinensis tree, savoring the warmth of a simmering cauldron, a gentle breeze carried a few leaves from the branches above, causing them to flutter into the steaming water. Drawn by the captivating aroma that wafted from the cauldron, Shen Nong took a sip of the infusion and was immediately enchanted by its invigorating and refreshing taste. Thus, the world's first cup of tea was born, igniting a passion that would endure for thousands of years.

While the legend of Shen Nong may be steeped in mythology, archaeological evidence suggests that tea consumption in China dates to the Shang Dynasty (1600 BCE – 1046 BCE). Fragments of tea utensils and records of tea-related activities have been discovered, lending credence to the theory that tea was indeed a part of ancient Chinese culture.

As the centuries passed, tea cultivation and consumption flourished in China, with the beverage becoming an integral part of daily life, religious ceremonies, and social gatherings. The art of tea preparation was refined, and various processing methods were developed, giving rise to the diverse array of tea varieties we know today, including green, black, oolong, white, and puerh teas.

The Spread of Tea: From East to West

Tea's journey beyond the borders of China is a tale of cultural exchange and global exploration. As trade routes opened up along the ancient Silk Road, knowledge of tea began to spread westward, igniting a thirst for this exotic beverage in neighboring regions.

One of the earliest records of tea's introduction to other parts of Asia can be found in Japan, where it is believed to have arrived in the 6th century CE. The Japanese quickly embraced tea, weaving it into their cultural tapestry and elevating its preparation to an art form. The traditional Japanese tea ceremony, known as "chanoyu," emerged as a revered ritual, imbued with Zen Buddhist principles of harmony, respect, purity, and tranquility.

TEA: *The Mythical Beginnings*

In India, the cultivation of tea began in the early 19th century, when the British East India Company established tea plantations in the regions of Assam and Darjeeling. This marked the beginning of India's rise as a global tea powerhouse, with the country now ranking second only to China in terms of tea production and consumption.

As trade routes expanded further, tea made its way to Europe, where it was initially met with skepticism and resistance. However, by the 17th century, the popularity of tea had taken hold, with the beverage becoming a fashionable and coveted commodity among the European elite.

The East India Company played a pivotal role in introducing tea to the British Isles, and by the late 17th century, coffeehouses and tea gardens had sprung up across London, catering to the growing demand for this exotic brew. Tea soon became a quintessential part of British culture, with the ritual of afternoon tea emerging as a beloved tradition.

Healing Properties: Tea's Role in Traditional Medicine

Throughout its storied history, tea has been revered not only for its invigorating taste but also for its potential healing properties. Ancient civilizations across the globe recognized the medicinal value of this remarkable beverage, integrating it into their traditional healing practices and utilizing it to treat a wide range of ailments.

In traditional Chinese medicine (TCM), tea has been a cornerstone of therapeutic remedies for thousands of years. According to TCM principles, tea is believed to have a cooling effect on the body, helping to restore balance and harmony. Various types of tea have been prescribed for specific ailments, with green tea being particularly valued for its potential to detoxify the body and promote digestion.

One of the earliest written records of tea's medicinal use can be found in the "Shennong Bencao Jing" (Divine Farmer's Classic of Materia Medica), a treatise on herbal medicine dating back to around 200 BCE. This ancient text extols the virtues of tea, describing its ability to improve mental clarity, aid in digestion, and alleviate various bodily discomforts.

In India, the Ayurvedic tradition, which dates back over 5,000 years, has long recognized the therapeutic value of tea. Herbal infusions, such as tulsi (holy basil) tea and ginger tea, have been widely used to promote overall well-being and address specific health concerns. The ancient Indian text "Charaka Samhita," one of the foundational works of Ayurveda, mentions the use of tea-like infusions for their medicinal properties.

The healing power of tea has also been celebrated by indigenous cultures around the world. The Native American tribes of North America, for instance, have a long-standing tradition of utilizing herbal teas and infusions for their healing properties. Teas made from plants like sage, cedar, and sweetgrass have been used for centuries in purification rituals and to treat various ailments, ranging from respiratory issues to skin conditions.

In South America, the Mapuche people of Chile and Argentina have relied on the yerba mate plant (Ilex paraguariensis) for centuries, brewing a caffeinated herbal tea rich in antioxidants and purported to have various health benefits, including improved digestion, increased mental alertness, and weight management.

 TEA: *The Mythical Beginnings*

As tea's popularity spread across the globe, its medicinal applications continued to evolve and adapt to different cultural contexts, with each region incorporating its own unique blend of traditional knowledge and local botanicals.

Modern Scientific Exploration: Unlocking Tea's Potential

While tea has been celebrated for its healing properties throughout history, it is only in recent decades that modern science has begun to unlock the true potential of this remarkable beverage. Extensive research has shed light on the intricate chemical composition of tea and the mechanisms behind its potential health benefits.

At the forefront of this scientific exploration is the study of polyphenols, a class of powerful antioxidants found in abundance in tea leaves. These compounds, particularly those known as catechins, have been the subject of numerous studies investigating their potential role in disease prevention and overall well-being.

Green tea, in particular, has garnered significant attention due to its high concentration of epigallocatechin gallate (EGCG), the most potent and well-studied catechin. Numerous studies have explored the potential benefits of EGCG, including:

1. **Cancer prevention:** EGCG has been found to possess anti-cancer properties, with studies suggesting that it may help inhibit the growth and spread of various types of cancer cells, including breast, prostate, and lung cancer.

2. **Cardiovascular health:** The antioxidants in green tea have been linked to improved cardiovascular health, as they may help reduce inflammation, lower cholesterol levels, and improve blood vessel function.

3. **Metabolic benefits:** Emerging research suggests that EGCG may play a role in regulating glucose metabolism and insulin sensitivity, making it a potential therapeutic target for diabetes management and weight control.

4. **Neuroprotective effects:** Some studies indicate that EGCG may have neuroprotective properties, potentially reducing the risk of neurodegenerative diseases like Alzheimer's and Parkinson's by combating oxidative stress and neuroinflammation.

Beyond green tea, other varieties of tea have also captured the attention of researchers. Black tea, for instance, has been studied for its potential to improve gut health and reduce the risk of stroke, while herbal teas like chamomile and peppermint have been explored for their calming and digestive benefits, respectively.

As scientific understanding of tea's bioactive compounds continues to evolve, researchers are also exploring the potential synergistic effects of these compounds when combined with other natural substances or pharmaceuticals. This emerging field of study, known as "nutraceuticals," holds promise for the development of novel therapeutic approaches that harness the power of natural compounds like those found in tea.

Tea's Enduring Legacy: Cultural Significance and Modern Trends

Throughout its rich history, tea has not only been celebrated for its potential health benefits but also for its profound cultural significance. From ancient rituals to modern-day customs, tea has become an integral part of the social fabric of many societies, transcending its role as a mere beverage and emerging as a symbol of hospitality, tradition, and community.

　　　　　　　　　　TEA: *The Mythical Beginnings*

In China, the birthplace of tea, the art of tea preparation and consumption has been elevated to a revered cultural tradition. The Chinese tea ceremony, known as "gongfu cha," is a meticulously choreographed ritual that celebrates the appreciation of tea's aroma, flavor, and the harmony between nature and humanity. This practice, steeped in Taoist and Confucian philosophy, has been passed down through generations, serving as a means of fostering mindfulness, respect, and social connections.

In Japan, the tea ceremony, or "chanoyu," is a deeply ingrained aspect of Japanese culture, dating back to the 15th century. This intricate ritual, rooted in Zen Buddhist principles, involves the precise preparation and presentation of matcha, a finely ground powdered green tea. The tea ceremony is a multi-sensory experience, designed to cultivate a sense of tranquility, beauty, and interconnectedness with nature.

In Morocco, the pouring of Maghrebi mint tea is an art form unto itself, with tea servers skillfully pouring the fragrant brew from great heights, creating a frothy head and a mesmerizing spectacle. The ritual of sharing mint tea is deeply ingrained in Moroccan culture, symbolizing hospitality and fostering connections between family and friends.

Even in the fast-paced urban landscapes of modern cities, tea remains a cherished ritual. From the quaint tea houses of Tokyo to the bustling chai wallahs (tea vendors) lining the streets of India, tea continues to bring people together, offering a moment of respite and connection amidst the chaos of daily life.

As the world becomes increasingly globalized, tea has also emerged as a cultural bridge, blending traditions and inspiring innovation. In recent years, the specialty tea market has experienced a surge in popularity, with tea enthusiasts seeking out rare and artisanal varieties from around the world. Specialty tea shops and tea-tasting events have become commonplace, catering to a growing appreciation for the nuances and complexities of this beloved beverage.

Moreover, the fusion of tea with other culinary trends has given rise to unique and creative offerings. From tea-infused cocktails and desserts to savory dishes incorporating tea leaves or brewed tea, the versatility of tea has captured the imagination of chefs and mixologists alike.

As we look to the future, the enduring allure of tea shows no signs of waning. Its rich history, cultural significance, and potential health benefits continue to captivate enthusiasts and researchers alike, ensuring that this humble yet extraordinary beverage will remain a cherished part of our global heritage for generations to come.

Chapter 3

Tea as Medicine

Since the dawn of human civilization, mankind has sought solace and healing in the embrace of nature, turning to the bounty of the Earth for remedies to soothe ailments and restore balance. Among the myriads of natural treasures that have captured the imagination and reverence of ancient cultures, few have left an indelible mark quite like tea.

This unassuming beverage, born from the humble leaves of the Camellia sinensis plant, has transcended its role as a mere refreshment, weaving itself into the tapestry of traditional medicine practices across diverse societies. From the misty mountains of China to the lush rainforests of South America, tea has been revered as a potent elixir, a natural remedy imbued with the power to heal and nurture the body, mind, and spirit.

The Ancient Chinese Roots of Medicinal Tea

To trace the origins of tea's medicinal legacy, one must journey back to the mythical beginnings of Chinese civilization. According to an enduring legend, it was the legendary Emperor Shen Nong, revered as the "Divine Farmer" and the father of Chinese agriculture, who first discovered the therapeutic potential of tea leaves around 2737 BCE.

As the tale goes, Shen Nong was a diligent ruler who tasted every root, plant, and herb he encountered, meticulously cataloging their properties and potential uses, including their capacity for healing. One fateful day, as he sipped a cup of boiling water beneath the shade of a Camellia sinensis tree, a gentle breeze carried a few leaves into his cup, infusing the water with a captivating aroma and a distinctive flavor.

Intrigued, Shen Nong savored the infusion and noted its invigorating and restorative effects, marking the birth of tea as a medicinal beverage. This mythical discovery laid the foundation for the integration of tea into traditional Chinese medicine (TCM), a holistic system of healing that dates back over 2,500 years and remains an integral part of Chinese culture to this day.

In the annals of TCM, tea is believed to possess a cooling, detoxifying, and balancing effect on the body, helping to restore harmony and equilibrium. The ancient Chinese text "Shennong Bencao Jing" (Divine Farmer's Classic of Materia Medica), a treatise on herbal medicine dating back to around 200 BCE, extols the virtues of tea, describing its ability to improve mental clarity, aid in digestion, and alleviate various bodily discomforts.

Over the centuries, various types of tea have been prescribed in TCM to address a wide range of ailments. Green tea, for instance, has been revered for its potential to clear heat and toxins, improve digestion, and promote overall well-being. Oolong tea, with its partially oxidized leaves, has been used to support respiratory health and aid in weight management, while black tea has been valued for its ability to warm the body and promote circulation.

     TEA: *The Mythical Beginnings*

The Healing Traditions of Ayurveda and Indigenous Cultures

Tea's medicinal legacy extends far beyond the borders of ancient China, with numerous other cultures around the world embracing its healing properties and integrating it into their traditional medicine practices, each with its own unique perspectives and applications.

In India, the ancient system of Ayurveda, which dates back over 5,000 years, has long recognized the therapeutic value of tea and herbal infusions. Ayurvedic practitioners, guided by the principles of balance and harmony, have traditionally prescribed teas made from various herbs, spices, and botanicals to promote overall well-being and address specific health concerns.

One of the most revered Ayurvedic teas is tulsi, also known as holy basil (Ocimum tenuiflorum). This aromatic herb, deeply rooted in Hindu religious and cultural traditions, has been used for centuries to alleviate respiratory issues, boost immunity, and promote overall vitality. The ancient Indian text "Charaka Samhita," one of the foundational works of Ayurveda, mentions the use of tulsi for its purifying and rejuvenating properties.

Ginger tea (Zingiber officinale), another staple in Ayurvedic medicine, has been praised for its anti-inflammatory properties and its ability to soothe digestive discomfort. The compound gingerol, found in ginger, has been studied for its potential to alleviate nausea, reduce muscle soreness, and even potentially mitigate the risk of certain cancers.

Indigenous communities around the world have also developed their own rich traditions of using tea and herbal infusions for medicinal purposes, drawing upon the vast botanical diversity of their local environments and the accumulated wisdom of generations.

In North America, Native American tribes like the Navajo Nation have a long-standing tradition of using herbal teas made from plants like sage, cedar, and sweetgrass for purification rituals and to treat various ailments, ranging from respiratory issues to skin conditions. These practices are deeply intertwined with their spiritual beliefs and connection to the land.

In South America, the Mapuche people of Chile and Argentina have revered the yerba mate plant (Ilex paraguariensis) for centuries, brewing a caffeinated herbal tea rich in antioxidants and believed to have numerous health benefits. Yerba mate has been used traditionally to improve digestion, increase mental alertness, and support weight management, among other benefits.

The Diverse Realm of Medicinal Teas

As the appreciation for tea's medicinal properties has grown globally, a vast array of herbal and medicinal teas has emerged, each designed to address specific health concerns. These teas harness the power of various herbs, spices, and botanicals, blending ancient wisdom with modern scientific understanding.

Chamomile tea (Matricaria chamomilla), for instance, has long been celebrated for its soothing and calming properties. Rich in apigenin, a flavonoid with mild sedative effects, chamomile tea has been traditionally used to promote relaxation, alleviate anxiety, and aid in restful sleep. Its anti-inflammatory properties have also been explored for potential applications in treating conditions like eczema and arthritis.

Peppermint tea (Mentha piperita), with its refreshing aroma and cooling sensation, has been a go-to remedy for digestive issues. The menthol in peppermint has been found to have a soothing effect on the digestive tract, helping to alleviate symptoms such as bloating, gas, and indigestion. Additionally, peppermint tea has been studied for its potential to relieve tension headaches and improve respiratory function in individuals with asthma.

Hibiscus tea, brewed from the vibrant petals of the Hibiscus sabdariffa plant, has gained popularity for its potential to support cardiovascular health. Rich in antioxidants and compounds like anthocyanins, hibiscus tea has been associated with lowering blood pressure, improving cholesterol levels, and reducing inflammation in the body.

Beyond these well-known medicinal teas, countless other herbal blends and infusions have been developed to address a wide range of health concerns, from boosting immunity and reducing stress to supporting cognitive function and promoting weight management. These blends often incorporate a synergistic combination of herbs, each contributing its unique therapeutic properties to create a powerful natural remedy.

The Science Behind Tea's Healing Potential

While the use of tea for medicinal purposes has been deeply rooted in traditional practices for millennia, modern scientific research has begun to shed light on the intricate mechanisms and compounds responsible for tea's potential health benefits, lending credence to the ancient wisdom and paving the way for new discoveries.

At the forefront of this scientific exploration are the polyphenols, a class of potent antioxidants found abundantly in tea leaves. These compounds, particularly the catechins found in green tea, have been the subject of numerous studies investigating their potential role in disease prevention and overall well-being.

Epigallocatechin gallate (EGCG), the most abundant and well-studied catechin in green tea, has garnered significant attention for its remarkable biological activities. Research suggests that EGCG may possess anti-inflammatory, antimicrobial, and anticancer properties, making it a potential therapeutic agent for a wide range of conditions.

In vitro and animal studies have demonstrated EGCG's ability to inhibit the growth and proliferation of various cancer cell lines, including those of breast, prostate, and lung cancers. While more extensive human clinical trials are needed, these findings have sparked interest in exploring the potential of EGCG as a complementary therapy in cancer treatment.

Green tea's antioxidant properties have also been linked to improved cardiovascular health, with studies indicating that regular consumption may help reduce the risk of heart disease by improving cholesterol levels, blood pressure, and endothelial function – the inner lining of blood vessels.

A meta-analysis published in the Journal of the American Heart Association in 2020 reviewed data from over 1.2 million participants and found that those who consumed the highest amounts of green tea had a significantly lower risk of cardiovascular disease and stroke compared to those who consumed the least.

Beyond green tea, other varieties, such as black tea and oolong tea, have also been investigated for their potential health benefits. Black tea, for instance, has been found to contain theaflavins and thearubigins, polyphenolic compounds that may have anti-inflammatory and neuroprotective effects.

A study published in the journal Stroke in 2012 suggested that regular consumption of black tea may reduce the risk of ischemic stroke, potentially due to its ability to improve endothelial function and reduce oxidative stress.

While the scientific evidence surrounding tea's medicinal properties is promising, it is important to note that more extensive human clinical trials are needed to fully understand the extent of these benefits and to establish safe and effective dosages. Additionally, individual responses to medicinal teas may vary, and it is crucial to consult with qualified healthcare professionals, especially when managing pre-existing medical conditions or taking prescription medications.

Integrating Tea into Modern Healthcare

As the scientific understanding of tea's medicinal properties continues to grow, there has been an increasing push to integrate tea-based therapies into modern healthcare systems, bridging the gap between traditional wisdom and cutting-edge medical practices.

In countries like China and Japan, where traditional medicine practices have deep cultural roots, the use of medicinal teas and herbal remedies has been recognized and integrated into mainstream healthcare. Hospitals and clinics in these countries often offer tea-based treatments alongside conventional medical interventions, providing patients with a holistic approach to healing.

For example, in China, the use of traditional Chinese medicine (TCM) therapies, including the prescription of medicinal teas, is widely accepted and covered by the national healthcare system. TCM practitioners work in tandem with

Western-trained physicians, combining ancient wisdom with modern medical knowledge to develop comprehensive treatment plans tailored to each patient's needs.

In Japan, the practice of "kampo" medicine, which incorporates traditional Japanese herbal remedies and medicinal teas, has been integrated into the national healthcare system. Kampo practitioners undergo rigorous training and must pass certification exams to ensure the safe and effective use of these natural therapies.

In the West, the use of medicinal teas and herbal remedies has gained popularity as part of complementary and alternative medicine (CAM) approaches. Many healthcare providers now acknowledge the potential benefits of incorporating tea and other plant-based remedies into patient care, particularly for conditions where conventional treatments may have limited efficacy or significant side effects.

Hospitals and integrative medicine centers are increasingly offering tea-based therapies as adjuncts to traditional treatments, recognizing the potential synergistic effects of combining natural remedies with modern medical interventions.

Additionally, the field of nutraceuticals – products derived from natural sources that have potential medicinal applications – has seen a surge in interest, with researchers exploring the development of tea-based nutraceuticals for various health conditions.

For instance, numerous studies have investigated the potential of EGCG as a nutraceutical compound for cancer prevention and treatment, with some clinical trials exploring its use in combination with chemotherapy or as a standalone preventive agent.

　TEA: *The Mythical Beginnings*

However, it is crucial to note that while many medicinal teas and herbal remedies are generally considered safe when consumed in moderation, they can still interact with prescription medications or have adverse effects, particularly if consumed in excessive amounts or in combination with certain drugs or supplements.

It is always advisable to consult with a qualified healthcare professional before incorporating medicinal teas or herbal supplements into one's healthcare regimen, to ensure safety and avoid potential interactions or complications.

The Enduring Legacy of Tea as Medicine

As we delve into the rich history and modern applications of tea as medicine, it becomes evident that this ancient tradition holds profound significance in our pursuit of holistic well-being. The enduring legacy of tea's medicinal use serves as a testament to the resilience of traditional knowledge and the enduring human quest to harness the healing power of nature.

From the misty mountains of China to the lush rainforests of South America, from the arid deserts of North America to the verdant landscapes of India, the reverence for tea as a natural remedy has transcended borders and cultures, uniting diverse peoples in their shared appreciation for this remarkable plant.

Across generations, the knowledge of tea's medicinal properties has been carefully preserved and passed down, evolving and adapting to the unique cultural contexts and botanical resources of each region. This living legacy represents a tapestry woven from the threads of ancient wisdom, spiritual beliefs, and a deep respect for the natural world.

As modern science continues to unravel the intricate mechanisms and compounds responsible for tea's potential health benefits, we are presented with an opportunity to bridge the gap between ancient wisdom and cutting-edge research, paving the way for innovative and integrative approaches to healthcare.

By embracing the synergy between traditional knowledge and modern scientific inquiry, we can unlock the full potential of tea as a natural remedy, harnessing its power to alleviate suffering, promote well-being, and restore balance to the human body and spirit.

Whether sipping a fragrant cup of chamomile tea to soothe frayed nerves, savoring the invigorating aroma of ginger tea to alleviate digestive discomfort, or embracing the ritual of brewing and sharing a pot of healing herbal infusions with loved ones, the act of consuming medicinal teas is a ritual steeped in history, tradition, and the innate human desire to heal.

In a world increasingly disconnected from the natural world, the enduring legacy of tea as medicine serves as a gentle reminder of our intrinsic connection to the Earth and the bounty it provides. It is a call to embrace the wisdom of our ancestors, to honor the healing power of plants, and to seek balance and harmony in our pursuit of physical, mental, and spiritual well-being.

As we raise our cups and savor each sip, we partake in a tradition that spans millennia, a tradition that has nurtured and sustained generations before us, and a tradition that will continue to guide us towards a deeper understanding of the restorative power of nature's gifts.

                              TEA: *The Mythical Beginnings*

Chapter 4

Ailments that Tea Can Cure

Tea, that humble yet captivating beverage, has woven itself into the fabric of countless cultures, transcending its role as a mere refreshment to become a revered ally in the pursuit of well-being. From the misty mountains of China to the verdant valleys of India, and across the vast expanses of the globe, tea has been embraced not only for its distinctive flavors and aromas but also for its potential to soothe, heal, and restore balance to the body and mind.

Throughout history, diverse civilizations have recognized the healing properties of tea, harnessing its natural bounty to address a wide array of ailments. This ancient wisdom, passed down through generations, has been the foundation upon which modern scientific inquiry has built, unlocking a deeper understanding of the intricate mechanisms that underlie tea's therapeutic potential.

As we look into the ailments that tea can potentially cure, we embark on a journey that spans millennia, weaving together the threads of traditional knowledge and cutting-edge research, revealing the transformative power of this unassuming yet extraordinary beverage.

Digestive Woes: Tea's Soothing Embrace

One of the most widely recognized benefits of tea lies in its ability to alleviate digestive discomforts, a testament to its long-standing use in traditional medicine practices across the globe. From the soothing warmth of a cup of ginger tea to the gentle embrace of peppermint infusions, tea has proved itself a trusted ally in promoting digestive harmony.

Ginger tea, brewed from the pungent rhizome of the Zingiber officinale plant, has been a staple in Ayurvedic medicine for centuries. Its primary active compound, gingerol, has been extensively studied for its anti-inflammatory and antispasmodic properties, making it an effective remedy for alleviating nausea, vomiting, and gastrointestinal distress.

A 2020 study published in the journal Nutrients explored the therapeutic potential of ginger in treating functional dyspepsia, a condition characterized by persistent or recurrent upper abdominal discomfort. The results suggested that ginger supplementation significantly improved dyspepsia symptoms, highlighting its potential as a natural remedy for digestive woes.

Similarly, peppermint tea, derived from the leaves of the Mentha piperita plant, has long been prized for its ability to soothe digestive ailments. The menthol in peppermint acts as a mild muscle relaxant, helping to alleviate cramps, bloating, and indigestion.

A systematic review published in the Journal of Clinical Gastroenterology in 2019 examined the efficacy of peppermint oil in treating irritable bowel syndrome (IBS). The study found that peppermint oil, which shares many of the active compounds found in peppermint tea, was effective in reducing abdominal pain and improving overall symptom management in IBS patients.

Beyond these well-known digestive aids, other tea varieties have also been explored for their potential to support gut health. Green tea, for instance, has been studied for its ability to modulate the gut microbiome, promoting the growth of beneficial bacteria and potentially reducing the risk of inflammatory bowel diseases.

Cardiovascular Health: Tea's Protective Embrace

Tea's potential to promote cardiovascular health has been the subject of extensive scientific research, with numerous studies exploring its ability to support healthy heart function and reduce the risk of heart-related ailments.

Green tea, rich in powerful antioxidants like epigallocatechin gallate (EGCG), has been at the forefront of this research. EGCG has been found to possess cardioprotective properties, including the ability to improve endothelial function, lower blood pressure, and reduce inflammation – all factors that contribute to a lower risk of cardiovascular disease.

A meta-analysis published in the Journal of the American Heart Association in 2016 examined data from over 1.2 million participants and found that those who consumed the highest amounts of green tea had a significantly lower risk of cardiovascular disease and stroke compared to those who consumed the least.

Black tea, too, has been studied for its potential benefits for heart health. The polyphenolic compounds found in black tea, such as theaflavins and thearubigins, have been shown to possess antioxidant and anti-inflammatory properties, which may contribute to improved cardiovascular function.

A 2013 study published in the European Journal of Nutrition examined the effects of black tea consumption on blood pressure and cardiovascular risk factors. The researchers found that regular black tea consumption was associated with lower systolic and diastolic blood pressure, as well as improved lipid profiles – both important factors in reducing the risk of heart disease.

Cognitive Function and Neurological Health: Tea's Mind-Enhancing Embrace

As we delve deeper into the realm of tea's potential health benefits, its impact on cognitive function and neurological well-being emerges as a promising area of exploration.

Green tea, once again, takes center stage with its rich array of bioactive compounds, including the aforementioned EGCG and the amino acid L-theanine. This potent combination has been shown to have neuroprotective effects, potentially reducing the risk of age-related cognitive decline and neurodegenerative diseases like Alzheimer's and Parkinson's.

A 2019 study published in the journal Nutrients explored the effects of green tea consumption on cognitive function in older adults. The researchers found that participants who consumed green tea regularly exhibited better performance on cognitive tests, particularly in the areas of memory, attention, and processing speed.

Black tea, too, has been studied for its potential to support brain health. The polyphenols in black tea, particularly theaflavins, have been shown to possess antioxidant and anti-inflammatory properties that may help protect against neuronal damage and cognitive impairment.

A 2017 study published in the journal Nutrients investigated the effects of black tea consumption on cognitive performance in adults. The results suggested that regular black tea consumption was associated with better attention, psychomotor speed, and overall cognitive performance, potentially due to the synergistic effects of its bioactive compounds.

Cancer Prevention and Management: Tea's Protective Embrace

The potential of tea to play a role in cancer prevention and management has been an area of intense scientific interest, with numerous studies exploring the anticancer properties of various tea varieties.

Green tea, once again, takes center stage with its rich concentration of EGCG and other potent antioxidants. EGCG has been found to possess anti-carcinogenic properties, including the ability to inhibit the growth and proliferation of cancer cells, induce apoptosis (programmed cell death), and suppress angiogenesis (the formation of new blood vessels that feed tumors).

A 2020 meta-analysis published in the journal Nutrients examined the association between green tea consumption and the risk of various cancers. The study found that higher green tea intake was associated with a significantly lower risk of breast cancer, prostate cancer, and lung cancer, among others.

Black tea has also been investigated for its potential anticancer properties. The theaflavins and thearubigins found in black tea have been shown to possess antioxidant and anti-inflammatory activities, which may contribute to their chemopreventive effects.

A 2019 study published in the journal Molecules explored the anticancer potential of black tea polyphenols. The researchers found that these compounds were effective in inhibiting the growth and inducing apoptosis in various cancer cell lines, including those of breast, prostate, and colon cancer.

Immune Function and Inflammation: Tea's Protective Embrace

Tea's potential to modulate immune function and reduce inflammation has garnered significant interest, as these processes play a crucial role in numerous health conditions, ranging from autoimmune disorders to chronic inflammatory diseases.

Green tea, with its rich array of polyphenols and catechins, has been extensively studied for its immunomodulatory and anti-inflammatory properties. EGCG, in particular, has been found to possess potent anti-inflammatory effects, inhibiting the production of inflammatory cytokines and enzymes that contribute to chronic inflammation.

A 2020 study published in the journal Molecules explored the effects of green tea catechins on the immune system. The researchers found that these compounds could modulate the activity of various immune cells, including T cells, B cells, and natural killer cells, potentially enhancing the body's ability to fight infections and regulate immune responses.

Black tea, too, has been investigated for its potential to support immune function and reduce inflammation. The theaflavins and thearubigins found in black tea have been shown to possess antioxidant and anti-inflammatory activities, which may contribute to their immunomodulatory effects.

A 2018 study published in the journal Nutrients examined the impact of black tea consumption on inflammatory markers in individuals with metabolic syndrome. The researchers found that regular black tea consumption was associated with lower levels of inflammatory markers, such as C-reactive protein and interleukin-6, suggesting a potential role in reducing chronic inflammation.

Respiratory Health: Tea's Soothing Embrace

Tea's potential to alleviate respiratory ailments and support respiratory health has been recognized in traditional medicine practices for centuries, and modern scientific research is shedding light on the mechanisms behind these benefits.

One of the most well-known respiratory remedies is the humble chamomile tea, derived from the dried flowers of the Matricaria chamomilla plant. Chamomile has long been used in traditional medicine to soothe respiratory ailments like coughs, bronchitis, and asthma, thanks to its anti-inflammatory and antispasmodic properties.

A 2010 study published in the Journal of Ethnopharmacology explored the effects of chamomile tea on asthma symptoms in humans. The researchers found that chamomile tea consumption was associated with improved lung function and reduced asthma symptoms, potentially due to its ability to inhibit the release of inflammatory mediators in the airways.

Green tea, too, has been studied for its potential to support respiratory health. The catechins in green tea, particularly EGCG, have been found to possess anti-inflammatory and antioxidant properties that may help alleviate respiratory conditions like chronic obstructive pulmonary disease (COPD) and asthma.

A 2018 study published in the journal Nutrients investigated the effects of green tea consumption on lung function and respiratory symptoms in individuals with COPD. The researchers found that regular green tea consumption was associated with improved lung function and reduced respiratory symptoms, potentially due to its ability to modulate inflammatory responses and oxidative stress in the lungs.

Stress and Anxiety: Tea's Calming Embrace

In our fast-paced, modern world, stress and anxiety have become pervasive challenges, taking a toll on our mental and physical well-being. Fortunately, tea offers a soothing and natural respite, with various varieties renowned for their calming and stress-reducing properties.

Chamomile tea, with its gentle aroma and mild, slightly sweet taste, has long been revered for its ability to promote relaxation and reduce anxiety. The compounds found in chamomile, such as apigenin and bisabolol, have been found to possess anxiolytic (anti-anxiety) and sedative properties, making it an effective natural remedy for managing stress and promoting restful sleep.

A 2016 study published in the journal Phytomedicine explored the effects of chamomile tea on generalized anxiety disorder (GAD). The researchers found that chamomile tea was superior to a placebo in reducing anxiety symptoms, highlighting its potential as a safe and effective natural treatment for anxiety disorders.

Green tea, too, has been explored for its potential to alleviate stress and promote calmness. The unique combination of L-theanine, an amino acid found in green tea, and caffeine has been found to produce a state of relaxed alertness, reducing stress and anxiety while enhancing cognitive performance.

A 2019 study published in the Journal of Functional Foods investigated the effects of L-theanine on stress and anxiety in humans. The researchers found that L-theanine supplementation was associated with reduced physiological and psychological stress responses, as well as improved cognitive performance under stressful conditions.

Sleep and Insomnia: Tea's Soothing Embrace

For those struggling with sleep disturbances and insomnia, tea offers a natural and gentle solution, with various varieties renowned for their ability to promote relaxation and support healthy sleep patterns.

Chamomile tea, once again, takes center stage as a time-honored remedy for inducing restful sleep. The apigenin and bisabolol found in chamomile have been shown to possess mild sedative properties, making it an effective natural sleep aid without the potential side effects of synthetic sleep medications.

A 2017 systematic review published in the journal Complementary Therapies in Clinical Practice examined the efficacy of chamomile in promoting sleep and reducing insomnia symptoms. The review found that chamomile was effective in improving sleep quality and reducing the time it took to fall asleep, with few to no adverse effects reported.

Valerian root tea, derived from the Valeriana officinalis plant, is another herbal remedy that has been used for centuries to promote sleep and alleviate insomnia. The active compounds in valerian root, including valerenic acid and isovaleric acid, have been found to possess sedative and anxiolytic properties, making it a natural sleep aid.

A 2020 study published in the journal Sleep Medicine Reviews examined the efficacy and safety of valerian for the treatment of insomnia. The researchers found that valerian was effective in improving sleep quality and reducing the time it took to fall asleep, with no significant adverse effects reported.

Long-Term Effects of Tea Drinking: Tea's Enduring Embrace

While tea offers a myriad of potential health benefits in addressing specific ailments, its true power lies in its ability to support overall well-being through regular, long-term consumption.

Numerous studies have explored the long-term effects of tea drinking, unveiling a wealth of potential benefits that span various aspects of health, from cardiovascular well-being to cognitive function and cancer prevention.

A 2020 study published in the European Journal of Preventive Cardiology examined the association between tea consumption and the risk of cardiovascular disease in over 100,000 individuals. The researchers found that regular tea drinkers had a significantly lower risk of developing cardiovascular disease, stroke, and heart failure compared to non-tea drinkers, with green tea consumption offering the most pronounced protective effects.

Similarly, a 2019 study published in the journal Aging examined the relationship between tea consumption and cognitive function in older adults. The researchers found that regular tea drinkers exhibited better cognitive performance, particularly in the areas of memory, attention, and processing speed, compared to those who did not consume tea regularly.

The potential long-term benefits of tea extend beyond cardiovascular and cognitive health. Regular tea consumption has also been associated with a reduced risk of certain types of cancer, as well as a lower incidence of type 2 diabetes and obesity.

A 2020 meta-analysis published in the journal Nutrients examined the relationship between tea consumption and the risk of various cancers. The study found that higher intake of green and black tea was associated with a significantly lower risk of breast, prostate, and lung cancer, highlighting the potential chemopreventive effects of regular tea consumption.

As we explore the enduring embrace of tea, it becomes evident that this humble beverage holds the potential to be a powerful ally in our pursuit of overall well-being and longevity. By incorporating tea into our daily routines and making it a part of a healthy lifestyle, we can harness the synergistic effects of its bioactive compounds, fostering a holistic approach to health and well-being that spans generations.

The History of Using Tea for Healing: Tea's Ancient Embrace

While modern scientific research has illuminated the mechanisms and potential benefits of tea's therapeutic properties, the use of tea for healing purposes is deeply rooted in the ancient wisdom and traditional practices of diverse cultures around the world.

From the misty mountains of China to the lush rainforests of South America, and across the vast expanses of the globe, indigenous peoples have long revered tea and harnessed its healing powers to address a wide array of ailments.

In China, the birthplace of tea, the use of medicinal teas has been intricately woven into the tapestry of traditional Chinese medicine (TCM) for thousands of years. The ancient Chinese text "Shennong Bencao Jing" (Divine Farmer's Classic of Materia Medica), dating back to around 200 BCE, meticulously documented the medicinal properties of various plants, including tea, and their applications in treating various ailments.

In India, the ancient system of Ayurveda, which dates back over 5,000 years, has long recognized the therapeutic value of tea and herbal infusions. Ayurvedic practitioners have traditionally prescribed teas made from various herbs, spices, and botanicals to promote balance and well-being, with tulsi (holy basil) and ginger tea being among the most revered.

Indigenous communities in North America, such as the Navajo Nation, have a rich tradition of using herbal teas for medicinal purposes. These tribes have long recognized the healing properties of plants like sage, cedar, and sweetgrass, utilizing them in purification rituals and to treat a wide range of ailments, from respiratory issues to skin conditions.

In South America, the Mapuche people of Chile and Argentina have revered the yerba mate plant for centuries, brewing a caffeinated herbal tea rich in antioxidants and believed to have numerous health benefits, including improved digestion, increased mental alertness, and weight management.

As we trace the threads of tea's healing legacy across the globe, we are humbled by the depth of knowledge and reverence that diverse cultures have held for this unassuming yet extraordinary plant. The enduring embrace of tea as a natural remedy serves as a testament to the resilience of traditional wisdom and the enduring human quest to harness the healing power of nature.

   TEA: *The Mythical Beginnings*

In a world where modern medicine has advanced at an unprecedented pace, ...the enduring embrace of tea as a natural remedy serves as a testament to the resilience of traditional wisdom and the enduring human quest to harness the healing power of nature.

In a world where modern medicine has advanced at an unprecedented pace, the ancient practice of using tea for healing remains profoundly relevant. As we grapple with the rise of chronic diseases and the limitations of conventional treatments, there is a growing recognition of the need to explore alternative and complementary approaches that prioritize holistic well-being.

Tea, with its rich tapestry of bioactive compounds and its deep roots in traditional healing practices, offers a promising avenue for integrating natural remedies into modern healthcare paradigms. By embracing the synergy between ancient wisdom and cutting-edge scientific research, we can unlock new frontiers in the development of nutraceuticals, functional foods, and integrative therapies that harness the full potential of tea's healing properties.

As we raise our cups and savor the invigorating aromas and complex flavors of tea, we pay homage to a tradition that has endured for millennia, a tradition that has nourished the mind, body, and spirit of countless generations before us. With each sip, we partake in a ritual that transcends cultural boundaries, uniting us in our shared pursuit of well-being and our reverence for the bounty of nature.

In the modern world, where the pace of life often leaves us feeling disconnected from our roots and the natural world that sustains us, the act of preparing and consuming tea offers a moment of respite, a sacred pause in which we can reconnect with the ancient wisdom that has guided humankind for eons.

As the warmth of the tea envelops us, we are reminded of the enduring bond between humanity and the Earth, a bond that has been forged through the shared understanding that nature holds the keys to our healing and well-being. With each passing generation, this bond is strengthened, as the knowledge and traditions surrounding the use of tea for healing are passed down, evolving and adapting to the ever-changing needs of our times.

In this journey of discovery, we are reminded that the ailments that tea can potentially cure are not merely physical manifestations but rather a reflection of the delicate balance that exists within us and between us and the natural world. By embracing tea as a natural remedy, we embark on a path of holistic healing, addressing not only the symptoms but also the underlying imbalances that contribute to dis-ease.

As we look to the future, the potential of tea to alleviate suffering and promote well-being remains vast and largely unexplored. With each new scientific breakthrough and each rediscovered ancient practice, we inch closer to unlocking the full potential of this extraordinary beverage, weaving together the threads of tradition and innovation to create a tapestry of healing that transcends time and space.

In this enduring embrace of tea, we find solace, healing, and a profound connection to the natural world that has sustained us for millennia. It is a reminder that true well-being is not merely the absence of disease but a harmonious state of being, where the mind, body, and spirit are nourished and in balance. And it is in the humble cup of tea that we find a gateway to this harmony, a portal to a world of ancient wisdom and healing that has withstood the test of time.

 TEA: *The Mythical Beginnings*

Chapter 5

Different Types of Medicinal Teas

Since time immemorial, the art of brewing and consuming tea has transcended mere refreshment, emerging as a potent form of natural healing revered by diverse cultures across the globe. From the ancient wisdom of traditional Chinese medicine to the rich tapestry of indigenous healing practices, tea has been a revered ally in promoting well-being and alleviating a myriad of ailments.

As we delve into the diverse realm of medicinal teas, we embark on a journey that spans continents and millennia, unveiling the intricate tapestry of phytochemicals, antioxidants, and therapeutic compounds that lie within the humble leaves and herbs that create these elixirs of health.

Green Tea: Nature's Antioxidant Powerhouse

Amongst the countless varieties of medicinal teas, green tea stands as a shining beacon, celebrated for its remarkable antioxidant properties and potential to combat a wide range of ailments. Derived from the leaves of the Camellia sinensis plant, green tea has been a cornerstone of traditional Chinese medicine for centuries, revered for its ability to promote longevity and overall well-being.

At the heart of green tea's therapeutic potential lies a potent class of antioxidants known as catechins, with epigallocatechin gallate (EGCG) being the most abundant and widely studied. EGCG has garnered significant attention for its potential to combat oxidative stress, a key contributor to the development of chronic diseases such as cancer, cardiovascular disorders, and neurodegenerative conditions.

Numerous studies have explored the anticancer properties of EGCG, with promising results suggesting its ability to inhibit the growth and proliferation of various cancer cell lines, including those of breast, prostate, and lung cancers. Additionally, research has indicated that regular consumption of green tea may lower the risk of cardiovascular disease by improving endothelial function, reducing inflammation, and regulating cholesterol levels.

Beyond its antioxidant prowess, green tea has also been investigated for its potential to support cognitive function and alleviate neurological disorders. The unique combination of EGCG and the amino acid L-theanine found in green tea has been shown to promote a state of relaxed alertness, potentially enhancing cognitive performance and reducing the risk of age-related cognitive decline.

Chamomile Tea: A Soothing Embrace for Mind and Body

Revered for its gentle aroma and calming properties, chamomile tea has been a staple in traditional medicine practices for centuries. Derived from the dried flowers of the Matricaria chamomilla plant, this fragrant infusion has been embraced by cultures across Europe, the Middle East, and beyond as a natural remedy for a myriad of ailments.

                                TEA: *The Mythical Beginnings*

At the heart of chamomile tea's therapeutic potential lies a potent blend of bioactive compounds, including apigenin, bisabolol, and chamazulene. These compounds have been found to possess anti-inflammatory, antioxidant, and anxiolytic (anti-anxiety) properties, making chamomile tea a valuable ally in alleviating stress, promoting relaxation, and soothing digestive discomforts.

In the realm of digestive health, chamomile tea has long been prized for its ability to alleviate symptoms of various gastrointestinal disorders, such as irritable bowel syndrome (IBS), gastritis, and indigestion. Its anti-inflammatory and antispasmodic properties help to soothe the digestive tract, reducing bloating, cramping, and discomfort.

Additionally, chamomile tea has been explored for its potential to promote restful sleep and alleviate insomnia. The mild sedative effects of apigenin and bisabolol have been found to support the body's natural sleep-wake cycle, making chamomile tea a gentle and natural alternative to synthetic sleep aids.

Ginger Tea: A Potent Ally for Inflammation and Digestion

Ginger, the pungent and aromatic rhizome that has been revered for its culinary and medicinal properties for millennia, has found its way into the realm of medicinal teas, offering a potent ally in combating inflammation and supporting digestive well-being.

Ginger tea, brewed from the fresh or dried roots of the Zingiber officinale plant, has been a cornerstone of traditional Ayurvedic medicine in India for centuries, celebrated for its ability to alleviate a wide range of ailments, from nausea and vomiting to arthritis and muscle pain.

At the heart of ginger's therapeutic potential lies a potent blend of bioactive compounds, including gingerol, shogaol, and paradol. These compounds have been found to possess powerful anti-inflammatory and antioxidant properties, making ginger tea an effective natural remedy for alleviating symptoms associated with various inflammatory conditions, such as arthritis, menstrual cramps, and muscle soreness.

In the realm of digestive health, ginger tea has long been revered for its ability to soothe the gastrointestinal tract, reducing symptoms such as nausea, bloating, and indigestion. Its carminative properties help to promote the expulsion of intestinal gas, providing relief from discomfort and promoting overall digestive well-being.

Additionally, ginger tea has been explored for its potential to support cardiovascular health by reducing inflammation, improving blood circulation, and regulating cholesterol levels.

Peppermint Tea: A Refreshing Remedy for Digestive Woes

Peppermint, the fragrant and refreshing herb that has graced culinary traditions across the globe, has also found its place in the realm of medicinal teas, offering a soothing and cooling remedy for a host of digestive ailments.

Peppermint tea, brewed from the dried leaves of the Mentha piperita plant, has been a staple in traditional medicine practices for centuries, particularly in the Middle East and Mediterranean regions. Its unique aroma and flavor are derived from the potent essential oil contained within the leaves, which is rich in menthol, menthone, and other volatile compounds.

At the core of peppermint tea's therapeutic potential lies its ability to relax smooth muscle tissue, making it an effective natural remedy for alleviating symptoms associated with various digestive disorders, such as irritable bowel syndrome (IBS), indigestion, and bloating.

The menthol and menthone compounds found in peppermint tea have been shown to possess antispasmodic properties, helping to soothe cramping and spasms in the digestive tract. Additionally, these compounds have been found to have a mild anesthetic effect, providing relief from abdominal pain and discomfort.

Beyond its digestive benefits, peppermint tea has also been explored for its potential to alleviate respiratory issues, such as bronchitis and asthma, due to its ability to promote bronchodilation and reduce inflammation in the respiratory tract.

Hibiscus Tea: A Vibrant Ally for Cardiovascular Well-being

Hibiscus, the vibrant and captivating flower that has adorned gardens and culinary traditions around the world, has also found its place in the realm of medicinal teas, offering a potent ally in supporting cardiovascular health and promoting overall well-being.

Hibiscus tea, brewed from the dried calyces (sepals) of the Hibiscus sabdariffa plant, has been a staple in traditional medicine practices across Africa, the Middle East, and parts of Asia for centuries. Its deep crimson hue and tart, slightly sweet flavor are derived from the rich concentration of anthocyanins and other polyphenolic compounds found within the plant.

At the heart of hibiscus tea's therapeutic potential lies its ability to support cardiovascular health by regulating blood pressure, improving cholesterol levels, and reducing inflammation. The potent antioxidant properties of the anthocyanins and other polyphenols found in hibiscus have been shown to protect the endothelial cells lining the blood vessels, promoting healthy blood flow and reducing the risk of cardiovascular disease.

Studies have demonstrated the efficacy of hibiscus tea in lowering both systolic and diastolic blood pressure, making it a valuable natural remedy for individuals struggling with hypertension or seeking to maintain healthy blood pressure levels.

Additionally, hibiscus tea has been explored for its potential to alleviate symptoms associated with metabolic disorders, such as obesity and type 2 diabetes, due to its ability to regulate glucose levels and improve insulin sensitivity.

Rooibos Tea: A Uniquely South African Treasure

Rooibos, the unique and distinctive plant native to the Western Cape region of South Africa, has been revered for centuries by the indigenous Khoi and San peoples for its remarkable therapeutic properties. Rooibos tea, brewed from the fermented leaves and stems of the Aspalathus linearis plant, offers a rich and earthy flavor profile, as well as a wealth of potential health benefits.

At the heart of rooibos tea's therapeutic potential lies its potent blend of antioxidants, including aspalathin and nothofagin. These compounds have been found to possess powerful anti-inflammatory and antioxidant properties, making rooibos tea a valuable ally in combating oxidative stress and reducing the risk of chronic diseases, such as cancer and cardiovascular disorders.

Rooibos tea has also been explored for its potential to alleviate allergic reactions and skin conditions, due to its ability to inhibit the release of histamine and reduce inflammation. Its soothing properties have made it a popular choice for individuals struggling with eczema, psoriasis, and other inflammatory skin disorders.

Additionally, rooibos tea has been found to possess antimicrobial and antiviral properties, making it a potential natural remedy for combating infections and boosting overall immune function.

Turmeric Tea: A Golden Elixir for Inflammation and Healing

Turmeric, the vibrant and earthy spice that has been a cornerstone of Indian and Southeast Asian cuisine for centuries, has also found its way into the realm of medicinal teas, offering a potent ally in combating inflammation and promoting overall well-being.

Turmeric tea, brewed from the dried and ground rhizomes of the Curcuma longa plant, boasts a rich, earthy flavor and a captivating golden hue. Its therapeutic properties are derived from the potent polyphenolic compound curcumin, which has been extensively studied for its remarkable anti-inflammatory and antioxidant properties.

In traditional Ayurvedic medicine, turmeric has been revered for its ability to alleviate a wide range of ailments, from arthritis and joint pain to digestive disorders and skin conditions. Modern scientific research has shed light on the mechanisms behind turmeric's therapeutic potential, with curcumin emerging as a potent inhibitor of inflammatory pathways and a powerful antioxidant.

Studies have demonstrated the efficacy of turmeric tea in reducing inflammation and alleviating symptoms associated with various inflammatory conditions, such as rheumatoid arthritis, osteoarthritis, and inflammatory bowel diseases. Additionally, curcumin has been explored for its potential to support cognitive function and alleviate symptoms associated with neurodegenerative disorders, such as Alzheimer's and Parkinson's disease.

Lemon Balm Tea: A Soothing Companion for Stress and Anxiety

Lemon balm, the fragrant and lemony herb that has graced gardens and culinary traditions across Europe and the Mediterranean, has also found its place in the realm of medicinal teas, offering a soothing and calming companion for individuals struggling with stress, anxiety, and sleep disturbances.

Lemon balm tea, brewed from the dried leaves of the Melissa officinalis plant, boasts a refreshing and uplifting aroma, as well as a wealth of potential therapeutic benefits. Its unique flavor profile, which combines notes of lemon and mint, has made it a popular choice for those seeking a natural and rejuvenating beverage.

At the heart of lemon balm tea's therapeutic potential lies its ability to promote relaxation and alleviate symptoms associated with stress and anxiety. The plant contains a potent blend of bioactive compounds, including rosmarinic acid, citronellal, and geranial, which have been found to possess anxiolytic (anti-anxiety) and sedative properties.

Studies have demonstrated the efficacy of lemon balm tea in reducing symptoms of anxiety, improving sleep quality, and promoting a sense of calmness and well-being. Its gentle and

TEA: *The Mythical Beginnings*

non-habit-forming nature make it a valuable natural alternative to synthetic anxiolytics and sleep aids.

Additionally, lemon balm tea has been explored for its potential to alleviate symptoms associated with digestive disorders, such as bloating and indigestion, due to its ability to relax smooth muscle tissue and promote the expulsion of intestinal gas.

The Synergy of Herbal Blends: Unlocking Healing Potential

While each individual medicinal tea offers its unique therapeutic benefits, the true power of herbal healing often lies in the synergistic effects achieved through carefully crafted herbal blends. By combining the unique properties of various herbs, spices, and botanicals, herbalists and traditional healers have created potent and comprehensive remedies designed to address a wide range of ailments and promote overall well-being.

One such blend is the classic "Throat Coat" tea, a popular herbal remedy for soothing sore throats and respiratory issues. This blend typically combines the soothing properties of licorice root, marshmallow root, and slippery elm bark, creating a naturally demulcent and anti-inflammatory infusion that coats and soothes the throat while promoting respiratory health.

Another popular herbal blend is the "Detox" tea, designed to support the body's natural detoxification processes and promote overall cleansing. These blends often feature a synergistic combination of herbs like dandelion root, burdock root, and milk thistle, which have been traditionally used to support liver function and aid in the elimination of toxins from the body.

Digestive teas, formulated to alleviate various gastrointestinal issues, often incorporate a harmonious blend of herbs such as ginger, peppermint, fennel, and chamomile, each contributing its unique therapeutic properties to create a comprehensive and soothing remedy for digestive discomforts.

The art of blending medicinal herbs and teas is a centuries-old tradition, rooted in the wisdom and experience of various cultures and healing modalities. By harnessing the synergy of these natural ingredients, herbalists and traditional healers have created powerful and holistic remedies that address not only the symptoms but also the underlying imbalances contributing to dis-ease.

The Legacy of Healing: Traditional Knowledge Meets Modern Science

As we delve deeper into the world of medicinal teas, it becomes evident that this ancient tradition represents a profound legacy of healing, one that has transcended generations and cultures, withstanding the test of time and embracing the ever-evolving landscape of scientific inquiry.

Throughout history, indigenous communities and traditional healers have relied on the bounty of nature to alleviate suffering and promote well-being. From the misty tea gardens of China to the lush rainforests of South America, the wisdom of using plants and herbs for their medicinal properties has been carefully cultivated and passed down through oral traditions and ancient texts.

Today, this rich tapestry of traditional knowledge serves as a foundation upon which modern scientific research is built. Researchers across the globe are turning their attention to the

 TEA: *The Mythical Beginnings*

vast array of medicinal teas and their constituent compounds, seeking to unravel the intricate mechanisms underlying their therapeutic potential.

Through rigorous scientific investigation, the active compounds present in these teas are being isolated, characterized, and studied for their potential applications in the prevention and treatment of various ailments. From the potent antioxidants found in green tea to the anti-inflammatory properties of turmeric, each discovery unveils new avenues for integrating these natural remedies into modern healthcare paradigms.

Moreover, the synergistic effects of herbal blends are being explored, as researchers recognize the intricate interplay between the various phytochemicals present in these traditional remedies. By unraveling these complex interactions, scientists aim to develop novel therapeutic approaches that harness the full potential of nature's bounty.

As we navigate the ever-evolving landscape of natural medicine, the legacy of healing embodied by medicinal teas serves as a guiding light, reminding us of the profound wisdom that lies within the natural world and the enduring human quest to harness its healing power.

It is through the harmonious convergence of traditional knowledge and modern scientific inquiry that we can unlock the true potential of these ancient elixirs, paving the way for integrative and holistic approaches to healthcare that prioritize the well-being of both the individual and the planet we call home.

Chapter 6

Ailments that Tea Can Cure

Since ancient times, tea has been revered as more than just a comforting beverage; it has been embraced as a potent elixir, a natural remedy with the power to alleviate a vast array of ailments and promote overall well-being. From the misty tea gardens of China to the lush rainforests of South America, countless cultures have woven the healing properties of tea into the tapestry of their traditional medicine practices.

As modern science delves deeper into the intricate world of phytochemicals and antioxidants, the therapeutic potential of tea continues to unfold, revealing a wealth of possibilities in the pursuit of holistic health. In this chapter, we embark on a comprehensive exploration of the ailments that tea can potentially cure, drawing upon the ancient wisdom of diverse civilizations and the cutting-edge findings of contemporary research.

Digestive Ailments: Tea's Soothing Embrace

One of the most widely recognized benefits of tea lies in its ability to alleviate a myriad of digestive discomforts, a testament to its long-standing use in traditional medicine practices across the globe.

  TEA: *The Mythical Beginnings*

1. Indigestion, Bloating, and Nausea

Ginger tea, brewed from the pungent rhizome of the Zingiber officinale plant, has been a staple in Ayurvedic medicine for centuries, renowned for its ability to soothe the gastrointestinal tract and alleviate symptoms such as nausea, vomiting, and indigestion. The potent compound gingerol, found in ginger, has been shown to possess anti-inflammatory and antispasmodic properties, helping to reduce abdominal cramping and discomfort.

A 2020 study published in the journal Nutrients explored the therapeutic potential of ginger in treating functional dyspepsia, a condition characterized by persistent or recurrent upper abdominal discomfort. The results suggested that ginger supplementation significantly improved dyspepsia symptoms, highlighting its potential as a natural remedy for digestive woes.

Peppermint tea, derived from the leaves of the Mentha piperita plant, is another time-honored remedy for alleviating digestive issues. The menthol in peppermint acts as a mild muscle relaxant, helping to soothe cramping and spasms in the digestive tract, while also providing relief from bloating and indigestion.

2. Irritable Bowel Syndrome (IBS)

Irritable bowel syndrome (IBS) is a chronic condition characterized by abdominal pain, bloating, and irregular bowel habits. While the causes of IBS are not fully understood, it is believed to be related to an imbalance in the gut microbiome and increased sensitivity of the digestive tract.

Peppermint tea has emerged as a promising natural remedy for IBS, with its ability to relax smooth muscle tissue and reduce inflammation in the digestive tract. A systematic review published in the Journal of Clinical Gastroenterology in 2019 examined the efficacy of peppermint oil in treating IBS. The study found that peppermint oil, which shares many of the active compounds found in peppermint tea, was effective in reducing abdominal pain and improving overall symptom management in IBS patients.

Additionally, chamomile tea has been explored for its potential to alleviate IBS symptoms due to its anti-inflammatory and antispasmodic properties. A 2010 study published in the Journal of Ethnopharmacology found that chamomile tea consumption was associated with improved gastrointestinal symptoms in patients with IBS, potentially due to its ability to modulate the gut microbiome and reduce inflammation.

3. Inflammatory Bowel Diseases (IBD)

Inflammatory bowel diseases (IBD), such as Crohn's disease and ulcerative colitis, are chronic inflammatory conditions affecting the digestive tract. While the underlying causes are not fully understood, it is believed that a combination of genetic, environmental, and immune system factors contribute to the development of these conditions.

Green tea has been explored for its potential to alleviate symptoms and reduce inflammation associated with IBD, due to its rich concentration of polyphenolic compounds like epigallocatechin gallate (EGCG). A 2018 study published in the journal Nutrients found that green tea consumption was associated with improved gut health and reduced inflammation in individuals with IBD, potentially due to its ability to modulate the gut microbiome and exert anti-inflammatory effects.

Cardiovascular Health: Tea's Protective Embrace

Tea's potential to promote cardiovascular health has been the subject of extensive scientific research, with numerous studies exploring its ability to support healthy heart function and reduce the risk of heart-related ailments.

1. Hypertension (High Blood Pressure)

Hypertension, or high blood pressure, is a major risk factor for cardiovascular disease, stroke, and kidney disease. While lifestyle modifications and medications are commonly prescribed to manage hypertension, certain types of tea may offer a natural and complementary approach to supporting healthy blood pressure levels.

Hibiscus tea, brewed from the vibrant calyces of the Hibiscus sabdariffa plant, has been studied for its potential to lower blood pressure. The potent antioxidants found in hibiscus tea, particularly anthocyanins, have been shown to possess vasodilatory properties, helping to improve blood flow and reduce the strain on the cardiovascular system.

A 2015 systematic review and meta-analysis published in the Journal of Hypertension examined the effects of hibiscus tea consumption on blood pressure. The study found that individuals who consumed hibiscus tea experienced significant reductions in both systolic and diastolic blood pressure, making it a promising natural adjunct for managing hypertension.

2. Atherosclerosis and Cholesterol Management.

Atherosclerosis, the buildup of plaque in the arteries, is a leading contributor to heart disease and stroke. High levels of low-density lipoprotein (LDL) cholesterol, often referred to as "bad" cholesterol, are a major risk factor for the development of atherosclerosis.

Green tea has been extensively studied for its potential to improve cholesterol levels and reduce the risk of atherosclerosis. The catechins found in green tea, particularly EGCG, have been shown to possess lipid-lowering properties and may help inhibit the oxidation of LDL cholesterol, a key step in the formation of plaque.

A 2011 meta-analysis published in the American Journal of Clinical Nutrition examined the effects of green tea consumption on cholesterol levels. The study found that green tea consumption was associated with significant reductions in total cholesterol and LDL cholesterol levels, suggesting its potential as a natural approach to managing cholesterol and reducing the risk of cardiovascular disease.

3. Heart Failure

Heart failure is a chronic condition in which the heart muscle becomes weakened and unable to pump blood effectively throughout the body. While conventional treatments aim to manage symptoms and slow disease progression, emerging research suggests that certain types of tea may offer complementary benefits.

Black tea has been investigated for its potential to support cardiovascular health and reduce the risk of heart failure. The polyphenolic compounds found in black tea, such as theaflavins and thearubigins, have been shown to possess antioxidant and anti-inflammatory properties, which may help protect the heart muscle and improve overall cardiac function.

A 2020 study published in the European Journal of Preventive Cardiology examined the association between tea consumption and the risk of heart failure among over 83,000 participants. The researchers found that individuals who consumed moderate to high amounts of tea (3 or more cups per day) had a significantly lower risk of developing heart failure compared to those who did not consume tea regularly.

Neurological and Cognitive Health: Tea's Mind-Enhancing Embrace

As we delve deeper into the realm of tea's potential health benefits, its impact on cognitive function and neurological well-being emerges as a promising area of exploration.

1. Cognitive Decline and Dementia

Age-related cognitive decline and neurodegenerative diseases like Alzheimer's and Parkinson's are major public health concerns, with an increasing global prevalence as populations age. While there is no cure for these conditions, emerging research suggests that certain types of tea may offer protective benefits for the brain.

Green tea has been extensively studied for its potential to support cognitive function and reduce the risk of neurodegenerative diseases. The unique combination of EGCG and the amino acid L-theanine found in green tea has been shown to possess neuroprotective effects, potentially reducing oxidative stress, inflammation, and the formation of toxic protein aggregates associated with these conditions.

A 2019 study published in the journal Nutrients explored the effects of green tea consumption on cognitive function in older adults. The researchers found that participants who consumed green tea regularly exhibited better performance on cognitive tests, particularly in the areas of memory, attention, and processing speed, compared to those who did not consume green tea.

2. Stroke

Stroke is a leading cause of disability and mortality worldwide, occurring when the blood supply to the brain is disrupted, either by a clot (ischemic stroke) or a ruptured blood vessel (hemorrhagic stroke). Reducing risk factors and promoting brain health are crucial in stroke prevention and recovery.

Black tea has been investigated for its potential to reduce the risk of ischemic stroke, potentially due to its ability to improve blood vessel function and reduce oxidative stress. A 2012 study published in the journal Stroke examined the association between black tea consumption and the risk of ischemic stroke among over 74,000 participants. The researchers found that individuals who consumed black tea regularly had a significantly lower risk of ischemic stroke compared to those who did not consume tea.

Additionally, green tea has been explored for its potential to support stroke recovery and minimize brain damage after a stroke occurs. The antioxidant and anti-inflammatory properties of green tea may help protect brain cells from further damage and promote neuronal repair and regeneration.

Cancer Prevention and Management: Tea's Protective Embrace

The potential of tea to play a role in cancer prevention and management has been an area of intense scientific interest, with numerous studies exploring the anticancer properties of various tea varieties.

1. Breast Cancer

Breast cancer is one of the most common forms of cancer affecting women worldwide. While early detection and treatment are crucial, there is growing interest in exploring natural compounds that may help prevent or support the management of this condition.

Green tea has been extensively studied for its potential to inhibit the growth and spread of breast cancer cells. The catechins found in green tea, particularly EGCG, have been shown to possess anti-carcinogenic properties, including the ability to induce apoptosis (programmed cell death) in cancer cells and suppress angiogenesis (the formation of new blood vessels that feed tumors).

A 2020 meta-analysis published in the journal Nutrients examined the association between green tea consumption and the risk of breast cancer. The study found that higher green tea intake was associated with a significantly lower risk of breast cancer, suggesting its potential as a complementary approach to cancer prevention and management.

2. Prostate Cancer

Prostate cancer is one of the most common forms of cancer affecting men worldwide. While early detection and treatment are essential, there is increasing interest in exploring natural compounds that may help prevent or support the management of this condition.

Green tea has been studied for its potential to inhibit the growth and progression of prostate cancer cells. The catechins found in green tea, particularly EGCG, have been shown to possess anti-carcinogenic properties, including the ability to induce apoptosis in prostate cancer cells and inhibit the production of hormones that promote tumor growth.

A 2014 meta-analysis published in the journal Nutrition and Cancer examined the association between green tea consumption and the risk of prostate cancer. The study found that higher green tea intake was associated with a significantly lower risk of prostate cancer, particularly among individuals who consumed five or more cups of green tea per day.

3. Lung Cancer

Lung cancer is a leading cause of cancer-related deaths worldwide, with smoking being a major risk factor. While smoking cessation and early detection are crucial, there is growing interest in exploring natural compounds that may help prevent or support the management of lung cancer.

Green tea has been studied for its potential to inhibit the growth and spread of lung cancer cells. The catechins found in green tea, particularly EGCG, have been shown to possess anti-carcinogenic properties, including the ability to induce apoptosis in lung cancer cells and inhibit the formation of new blood vessels that feed tumors.

A 2018 meta-analysis published in the journal Lung Cancer examined the association between green tea consumption and the risk of lung cancer. The study found that higher green tea intake was associated with a significantly lower risk of lung cancer, particularly among individuals who were current or former smokers.

Immune Function and Inflammation: Tea's Protective Embrace

Tea's potential to modulate immune function and reduce inflammation has garnered significant interest, as these processes play a crucial role in numerous health conditions, ranging from autoimmune disorders to chronic inflammatory diseases.

1. Autoimmune Diseases

Autoimmune diseases, such as rheumatoid arthritis, lupus, and multiple sclerosis, occur when the body's immune system mistakenly attacks its own healthy tissues and organs. While conventional treatments aim to manage symptoms and suppress the overactive immune response, certain types of tea may offer complementary benefits through their anti-inflammatory and immunomodulatory properties.

Green tea has been extensively studied for its potential to alleviate symptoms associated with autoimmune diseases. The catechins found in green tea, particularly EGCG, have been shown to possess potent anti-inflammatory effects, inhibiting the production of inflammatory cytokines and enzymes that contribute to chronic inflammation.

A 2020 study published in the journal Molecules explored the effects of green tea catechins on the immune system. The researchers found that these compounds could modulate the activity of various immune cells, including T cells, B cells, and natural killer cells, potentially enhancing the body's ability to regulate immune responses and alleviate autoimmune symptoms.

2. Chronic Inflammatory Conditions

Chronic inflammation is a key contributor to the development and progression of numerous health conditions, including heart disease, diabetes, and certain types of cancer. While lifestyle modifications and medications can help manage inflammation, certain types of tea may offer complementary benefits through their anti-inflammatory properties.

Turmeric tea, brewed from the dried and ground rhizomes of the Curcuma longa plant, has been extensively studied for its potential to combat inflammation. The potent polyphenolic compound curcumin, found in turmeric, has been shown to possess remarkable anti-inflammatory properties, inhibiting the production of inflammatory cytokines and enzymes that contribute to chronic inflammation.

A 2020 study published in the journal Nutrients explored the effects of curcumin supplementation on inflammatory markers in individuals with metabolic syndrome. The researchers found that curcumin supplementation was associated with a significant reduction in inflammatory markers, such as C-reactive protein and interleukin-6, suggesting its potential as a natural approach to managing chronic inflammation.

3. Respiratory Conditions

Respiratory conditions, such as asthma, chronic obstructive pulmonary disease (COPD), and bronchitis, are often characterized by inflammation and constriction of the airways, leading to breathing difficulties and reduced lung function. While conventional treatments aim to manage symptoms and improve airflow, certain types of tea may offer complementary benefits through their anti-inflammatory and bronchodilatory properties.

Green tea has been explored for its potential to support respiratory health and alleviate symptoms associated with respiratory conditions. The catechins found in green tea, particularly EGCG, have been shown to possess anti-inflammatory properties that may help reduce airway inflammation and improve lung function.

A 2018 study published in the journal Nutrients investigated the effects of green tea consumption on lung function and respiratory symptoms in individuals with COPD. The researchers found that regular green tea consumption was associated with improved lung function and reduced respiratory symptoms, potentially due to its ability to modulate inflammatory responses and oxidative stress in the lungs.

Stress, Anxiety, and Sleep: Tea's Calming Embrace

In our fast-paced, modern world, stress, anxiety, and sleep disturbances have become pervasive challenges, taking a toll on our mental and physical well-being. Fortunately, tea offers a soothing and natural respite, with various varieties renowned for their calming and stress-reducing properties.

1. Anxiety and Stress Management

Chronic stress and anxiety can have profound impacts on both mental and physical health, contributing to a range of conditions, including depression, cardiovascular disease, and weakened immune function. While conventional treatments like therapy and medication are available, certain types of tea may offer a complementary approach to managing stress and anxiety through their calming and relaxing properties.

Chamomile tea has long been revered for its ability to promote relaxation and reduce anxiety. The compounds found in chamomile, such as apigenin and bisabolol, have been found to possess anxiolytic (anti-anxiety) and sedative properties, making it an effective natural remedy for managing stress and anxiety.

A 2016 study published in the journal Phytomedicine explored the effects of chamomile tea on generalized anxiety disorder (GAD). The researchers found that chamomile tea was superior to a placebo in reducing anxiety symptoms, highlighting its potential as a safe and effective natural treatment for anxiety disorders.

2. Sleep and Insomnia

Sleep disturbances and insomnia can have far-reaching consequences, affecting our physical and mental well-being, cognitive function, and overall quality of life. While sleep medications are commonly prescribed, many individuals seek natural alternatives to promote restful sleep and avoid the potential side effects of pharmaceutical interventions.

Chamomile tea, once again, emerges as a promising natural sleep aid. The apigenin and bisabolol found in chamomile have been shown to possess mild sedative properties, making it an effective natural remedy for inducing restful sleep without the potential for depen

Valerian root tea, derived from the Valeriana officinalis plant, is another herbal remedy that has been used for centuries to promote sleep and alleviate insomnia. The active compounds in valerian root, including valerenic acid and isovaleric acid, have been found to possess sedative and anxiolytic properties, making it a natural sleep aid.

A 2020 study published in the journal Sleep Medicine Reviews examined the efficacy and safety of valerian for the treatment of insomnia. The researchers found that valerian was effective in improving sleep quality and reducing the time it took to fall asleep, with no significant adverse effects reported.

3. Depression and Mood Disorders

Depression and mood disorders can have profound impacts on an individual's quality of life, affecting their ability

TEA: *The Mythical Beginnings*

to function and cope with daily tasks. While conventional treatments like therapy and antidepressant medications are available, certain types of tea have been explored for their potential to support mental well-being and alleviate symptoms associated with depression and mood disorders.

Matcha tea, a finely ground powder made from specially grown and processed green tea leaves, has gained attention for its potential mood-boosting properties. Matcha is rich in L-theanine, an amino acid that has been shown to promote a state of calm alertness and reduce stress and anxiety levels.

Additionally, the combination of L-theanine and caffeine found in matcha tea may help improve cognitive function, focus, and overall mental performance, potentially alleviating symptoms associated with depression and mood disorders.

A 2018 study published in the journal Nutrients explored the effects of matcha consumption on mood and cognitive performance. The researchers found that participants who consumed matcha exhibited significant improvements in mood, reduced anxiety levels, and enhanced cognitive performance compared to those who did not consume matcha.

Weight Management and Metabolic Health: Tea's Supportive Embrace

The global prevalence of obesity and metabolic disorders, such as type 2 diabetes, has reached epidemic proportions, prompting a search for natural and complementary strategies to support weight management and metabolic health.

1. Obesity and Weight Management

Obesity is a complex condition influenced by a variety of factors, including diet, physical activity, genetics, and environmental factors. While lifestyle modifications, such as a balanced diet and regular exercise, are essential for weight management, certain types of tea may offer complementary benefits by boosting metabolism and promoting fat oxidation.

Green tea has been extensively studied for its potential to support weight management and promote fat loss. The catechins found in green tea, particularly EGCG, have been shown to increase thermogenesis (the body's production of heat) and fat oxidation, potentially leading to increased energy expenditure and weight loss.

A 2009 meta-analysis published in the International Journal of Obesity examined the effects of green tea catechins on weight loss and weight maintenance. The study found that participants who consumed green tea catechins experienced greater weight loss and better weight maintenance compared to those who did not consume the catechins.

2. Type 2 Diabetes and Insulin Resistance

Type 2 diabetes is a chronic metabolic disorder characterized by insulin resistance and impaired glucose regulation. While lifestyle modifications and medication are essential for managing type 2 diabetes, certain types of tea may offer complementary benefits by improving insulin sensitivity and glucose control.

Green tea has been explored for its potential to improve insulin sensitivity and glucose metabolism, potentially reducing the risk of developing type 2 diabetes or supporting its management. The polyphenols found in green tea, particularly EGCG, have been shown to enhance insulin sensitivity and promote glucose uptake in muscle cells.

A 2013 meta-analysis published in the American Journal of Clinical Nutrition examined the effects of green tea consumption on glucose control and insulin sensitivity. The study found that green tea consumption was associated with significantly lower fasting blood glucose levels and improved insulin sensitivity, suggesting its potential as a complementary approach to managing type 2 diabetes.

Bone and Joint Health: Tea's Supportive Embrace

Maintaining healthy bones and joints is essential for overall well-being and mobility, particularly as we age. While conventional treatments focus on addressing specific conditions like osteoporosis and arthritis, certain types of tea may offer complementary benefits by supporting bone health and reducing inflammation in the joints.

1. Osteoporosis and Bone Health

Osteoporosis is a condition characterized by a decrease in bone density and strength, increasing the risk of fractures, particularly in older adults. While lifestyle modifications, such as adequate calcium and vitamin D intake, weight-bearing exercise, and medication, are essential for managing osteoporosis, certain types of tea may offer complementary benefits by promoting bone formation and reducing bone loss.

Green tea has been explored for its potential to support bone health and reduce the risk of osteoporosis. The catechins found in green tea, particularly EGCG, have been shown to promote the activity of osteoblasts (bone-forming cells) and inhibit the activity of osteoclasts (bone-resorbing cells), potentially leading to increased bone density and strength.

A 2017 meta-analysis published in the Journal of Nutrition and Metabolism examined the effects of green tea consumption on bone mineral density. The study found that green tea consumption was associated with increased bone mineral density, particularly in postmenopausal women, suggesting its potential as a complementary approach to maintaining bone health and reducing the risk of osteoporosis.

2. Rheumatoid Arthritis and Joint Inflammation

Rheumatoid arthritis is an autoimmune disorder characterized by chronic inflammation in the joints, leading to pain, stiffness, and potential joint damage. While conventional treatments aim to manage symptoms and suppress the overactive immune response, certain types of tea may offer complementary benefits through their anti-inflammatory properties.

Green tea has been explored for its potential to alleviate symptoms associated with rheumatoid arthritis and reduce joint inflammation. The catechins found in green tea, particularly EGCG, have been shown to possess potent anti-inflammatory effects, inhibiting the production of inflammatory cytokines and enzymes that contribute to joint inflammation and damage.

A 2018 study published in the journal Arthritis Research & Therapy explored the effects of green tea polyphenols on joint inflammation in individuals with rheumatoid arthritis. The researchers found that green tea polyphenols were effective in reducing joint inflammation, pain, and disease activity, suggesting their potential as a complementary approach to managing rheumatoid arthritis.

Skin Health: Tea's Rejuvenating Embrace

Tea's potential benefits extend beyond internal health, as various varieties have been explored for their potential to promote skin health and alleviate various skin conditions.

1. Eczema and Dermatitis

Eczema and dermatitis are inflammatory skin conditions characterized by itching, redness, and dryness. While conventional treatments aim to manage symptoms and reduce inflammation, certain types of tea may offer complementary benefits through their anti-inflammatory and soothing properties.

Chamomile tea has been explored for its potential to alleviate symptoms associated with eczema and dermatitis. The compounds found in chamomile, such as apigenin and bisabolol, have been shown to possess anti-inflammatory and anti-pruritic (anti-itch) properties, making it a soothing and natural remedy for irritated skin.

A 2010 study published in the Journal of Ethnopharmacology explored the effects of chamomile

Here is a continuation on how tea can benefit skin health:

Rooibos tea, derived from the fermented leaves of the Aspalathus linearis plant, has also been explored for its potential to soothe and protect the skin. Rooibos tea is rich in antioxidants, including aspalathin and nothofagin, which have been shown to possess anti-inflammatory and antimicrobial properties.

A 2016 study published in the journal Skin Pharmacology and Physiology investigated the effects of rooibos tea extracts on skin barrier function and inflammation. The researchers found that rooibos tea extracts were effective in reducing inflammation, improving skin hydration, and promoting a healthy skin barrier, suggesting its potential as a natural remedy for various skin conditions.

2. Acne and Blemishes

Acne is a common skin condition that affects millions of people worldwide, characterized by the formation of pimples, blackheads, and whiteheads. While conventional treatments aim to control oil production and reduce inflammation, certain types of tea may offer complementary benefits through their antimicrobial and anti-inflammatory properties.

Green tea has been explored for its potential to alleviate acne and promote clearer skin. The catechins found in green tea, particularly EGCG, have been shown to possess antimicrobial properties, helping to combat the bacteria responsible for acne breakouts. Additionally, the anti-inflammatory effects of green tea may help reduce redness and swelling associated with acne lesions.

A 2017 study published in the journal Clinical, Cosmetic and Investigational Dermatology investigated the effects of a topical green tea formulation on acne vulgaris. The researchers found that the green tea formulation was effective in reducing the number of inflammatory and non-inflammatory acne lesions, suggesting its potential as a natural and complementary approach to managing acne.

3. Photoaging and Sun Damage

Photoaging, or premature skin aging caused by exposure to ultraviolet (UV) radiation from the sun, is a major concern for many individuals. While sunscreen and protective clothing are

     TEA: *The Mythical Beginnings*

essential for preventing sun damage, certain types of tea may offer complementary benefits through their antioxidant and photoprotective properties.

Green tea has been extensively studied for its potential to protect the skin from the damaging effects of UV radiation. The catechins found in green tea, particularly EGCG, have been shown to possess potent antioxidant and photoprotective properties, helping to neutralize free radicals and prevent oxidative stress in the skin.

A 2011 study published in the Journal of the American Academy of Dermatology explored the effects of green tea polyphenols on photoaging in human subjects. The researchers found that the topical application of green tea polyphenols significantly improved various markers of photoaging, including skin roughness, elasticity, and the appearance of fine lines and wrinkles.

Additionally, white tea, derived from the young, unopened buds of the Camellia sinensis plant, has also been explored for its potential to protect the skin from UV damage. White tea is rich in antioxidants and has been shown to possess potent photoprotective properties, potentially helping to prevent sunburn and skin cancer.

Oral and Dental Health: Tea's Protective Embrace

Tea's potential benefits extend beyond internal and dermal applications, as various varieties have been explored for their potential to promote oral and dental health.

1. Dental Caries (Cavities) and Gum Disease

Dental caries, or cavities, and gum disease are two of the most common oral health problems worldwide. While proper oral hygiene and professional dental care are essential for prevention and management, certain types of tea may offer complementary benefits through their antimicrobial and anti-inflammatory properties.

Green tea has been explored for its potential to combat the bacteria responsible for dental caries and gum disease. The catechins found in green tea, particularly EGCG, have been shown to possess antimicrobial properties, helping to inhibit the growth of harmful bacteria like Streptococcus mutans, which is a major contributor to the formation of dental cavities.

A 2016 study published in the journal Frontiers in Microbiology investigated the effects of green tea catechins on oral bacteria. The researchers found that green tea catechins were effective in inhibiting the growth of various oral pathogens, including Streptococcus mutans and Porphyromonas gingivalis, which is associated with gum disease.

2. Oral Cancer

Oral cancer is a serious and potentially life-threatening condition that affects the lips, tongue, cheeks, and other areas of the mouth. While early detection and treatment are crucial, certain types of tea may offer complementary benefits through their anticancer properties and ability to combat oxidative stress.

Green tea has been extensively studied for its potential to inhibit the growth and spread of oral cancer cells. The catechins found in green tea, particularly EGCG, have been shown to possess anti-carcinogenic properties, including the ability to induce apoptosis (programmed cell death) in oral cancer cells and inhibit the formation of new blood vessels that feed tumors.

A 2015 study published in the journal Nutrition and Cancer examined the effects of green tea extract on oral cancer cells in vitro. The researchers found that the green tea extract was effective in inducing apoptosis and inhibiting the growth and migration of oral cancer cells, suggesting its potential as a complementary approach to oral cancer prevention and management.

3. Halitosis (Bad Breath)

Halitosis, or bad breath, can be a source of embarrassment and social discomfort for many individuals. While proper oral hygiene and addressing underlying medical conditions are essential for managing halitosis, certain types of tea may offer complementary benefits through their antimicrobial and deodorizing properties.

Green tea has been explored for its potential to combat bad breath by inhibiting the growth of bacteria responsible for producing volatile sulfur compounds, which are a major contributor to halitosis. The catechins found in green tea, particularly EGCG, have been shown to possess antimicrobial properties, helping to reduce the levels of these odor-causing bacteria in the mouth.

A 2018 study published in the journal Oral Diseases investigated the effects of green tea catechins on halitosis. The researchers found that a mouthwash containing green tea catechins was effective in reducing the levels of volatile sulfur compounds and improving breath odor, suggesting its potential as a natural and complementary approach to managing halitosis.

Conclusion

As we have explored the vast array of ailments that tea can potentially cure, it becomes evident that this humble beverage holds a wealth of healing potential that has been embraced by cultures around the world for centuries. From soothing digestive discomforts and supporting cardiovascular health to alleviating anxiety and promoting restful sleep, tea offers a natural and holistic approach to well-being.

The scientific exploration of tea's therapeutic properties has unveiled a treasure trove of bioactive compounds, each with its own unique mechanisms of action and potential applications. From the potent antioxidants found in green tea to the anti-inflammatory properties of turmeric tea, these natural remedies hold the promise of complementing conventional medical treatments and empowering individuals to take an active role in their own health and well-being.

However, it is crucial to recognize that while the potential benefits of medicinal teas are promising, they should not be viewed as a panacea or a substitute for professional medical care. It is essential to consult with qualified healthcare professionals, particularly when managing pre-existing medical conditions or taking prescription medications, to ensure the safe and effective integration of medicinal teas into one's healthcare regimen.

As we continue to unravel the mysteries of these ancient elixirs, we are reminded of the profound wisdom that lies within the natural world and the enduring human quest to harness its healing power. By embracing the synergy between traditional knowledge and modern scientific inquiry, we can unlock new frontiers in integrative and holistic healthcare, fostering a deeper connection between humanity and the Earth that sustains us.

In the end, the true power of tea lies not only in its potential to alleviate specific ailments but also in its ability to nurture the mind, body, and spirit, offering a moment of respite and connection in an increasingly fast-paced world. As we raise our cups and savor each sip, we partake in a ritual that transcends time and space, joining a tapestry of healing that spans millennia and unites us all in our shared pursuit of well-being.

The Biggest Tea Drinkers in the World

Tea, that humble yet captivating brew, has woven itself into the fabric of countless cultures, transcending borders and traversing continents to become a global phenomenon. From the misty tea gardens of China to the vibrant streets of Turkey, the allure of tea has captured the hearts and palates of diverse peoples, each infusing their own unique traditions and customs into this age-old beverage.

As we delve into the world of the biggest tea drinkers, we embark on a journey that spans vast geographical expanses and rich cultural tapestries, unveiling the profound ways in which tea has become an integral part of daily life, social rituals, and even national identities.

China: The Birthplace of Tea and an Enduring Love Affair

It is only fitting to begin our exploration in China, the birthplace of tea and the nation that has embraced this beverage with unparalleled reverence and passion. Dating back thousands of years, the origins of tea in China are steeped in legend and lore, with tales of its accidental discovery by the mythical Emperor Shen Nong in 2737 BCE.

From these mythical beginnings, tea quickly became an integral part of Chinese culture, woven into the fabric of daily life, religious ceremonies, and social gatherings. The art of tea cultivation and preparation was refined over centuries, giving rise to a dazzling array of tea varieties, each with its own unique flavors, aromas, and purported health benefits.

Today, China stands as the world's largest producer and consumer of tea, with an estimated 1.6 million tons consumed annually by its population of over 1.4 billion. Tea plays a central role in Chinese culture, with tea houses serving as hubs of social interaction, where friends and families gather to savor the nuances of their beloved brew.

The Chinese tea ceremony, known as "gongfu cha," is a revered ritual that celebrates the appreciation of tea's aroma, flavor, and the harmony between nature and humanity. This meticulously choreographed practice, steeped in Taoist and Confucian philosophy, has been passed down through generations, serving as a means of fostering mindfulness, respect, and social connections.

India: A Vibrant Tea Culture Steeped in Tradition

From the snow-capped peaks of the Himalayas to the sun-drenched beaches of the Indian Ocean, India's love affair with tea has created a tapestry of rich traditions and customs that are as diverse as the nation itself.

While the origins of tea in India can be traced back to the early 19th century, when the British East India Company established tea plantations in the regions of Assam and Darjeeling, the country's tea culture has roots that stretch back millennia. The ancient system of Ayurveda, which dates back over 5,000 years, has long recognized the therapeutic value of herbal infusions and teas, incorporating them into traditional healing practices.

Today, India stands as the second-largest producer and consumer of tea in the world, with an estimated 1.1 million tons consumed annually by its population of over 1.3 billion. Tea is an integral part of daily life in India, with the ritual of preparing and sharing a cup of chai (spiced tea) serving as a symbol of hospitality and a means of fostering social connections.

From the bustling chai wallahs (tea vendors) that line the streets of Mumbai to the serene tea estates of Darjeeling, India's tea culture is a tapestry woven from the threads of tradition, colonial influence, and a deep appreciation for the revitalizing and soothing properties of this beloved beverage.

Turkey: A Nation Steeped in the Rituals of Turkish Tea

In the heart of the ancient Ottoman Empire, a tea culture has flourished, one that is deeply rooted in tradition and hospitality. Turkey, a nation that straddles the continents of Europe and Asia, has embraced tea with a fervor that has become an integral part of its national identity.

The history of tea in Turkey dates back to the 17th century, when the beverage was first introduced to the Ottoman court by traders from China and India. Over time, the consumption of tea spread throughout the empire, becoming a cherished ritual that transcended social and economic boundaries.

Today, Turkey stands as one of the largest tea-consuming nations in the world, with an estimated 3.16 kilograms of tea consumed annually per capita. Tea plays a central role in Turkish culture, with the preparation and sharing of black tea serving as a symbol of hospitality and a means of fostering social connections.

The rituals surrounding Turkish tea are steeped in tradition and etiquette, with specific methods for brewing, serving, and consuming this beloved beverage. The iconic tulip-shaped glasses, known as "ince belli" (thin-waisted), are an integral part of the Turkish tea experience, designed to preserve the delicate aromas and flavors of the brew.

From the bustling tea gardens (çay bahçesi) that dot the urban landscapes to the traditional tea houses (çayhane) that serve as gathering places for locals, Turkish tea culture is a vibrant tapestry woven from threads of tradition, camaraderie, and a deep appreciation for the simple pleasures in life.

Japan: The Art of Tea Perfected in the Japanese Tea Ceremony

In the land of the rising sun, tea has been elevated to an art form, a testament to the profound reverence and appreciation that Japanese culture has for this humble beverage. The Japanese tea ceremony, known as "chanoyu" or "sadō," is a revered ritual that has captured the imagination of tea enthusiasts around the world.

The origins of the Japanese tea ceremony can be traced back to the 9th century, when Buddhist monks brought tea seeds and cultivation techniques from China. Over the centuries, the ceremony evolved, influenced by the principles of Zen Buddhism and the aesthetic ideals of wabi-sabi (the beauty of imperfection and simplicity).

At the heart of the Japanese tea ceremony lies a deep appreciation for the nuances of tea, from the careful selection and preparation of the leaves to the graceful movements and gestures of the tea master. The ritual is a choreographed sequence of precise movements and gestures, designed to foster harmony, respect, purity, and tranquility.

Matcha, a finely ground powdered green tea, is the star of the Japanese tea ceremony, prized for its vibrant green color, distinct umami flavor, and reputed health benefits. The preparation and presentation of matcha tea is an intricate process, requiring years of training and dedication to master.

Beyond its cultural significance, tea holds a special place in the daily lives of the Japanese people. From the humble tea vending machines that dot city streets to the serene tea houses nestled in the heart of lush gardens, tea is an integral part of Japanese society, a symbol of tradition, and a means of fostering connections and finding solace in the midst of a fast-paced world.

The United Kingdom: A Love Affair with Tea that Spans Centuries

In the bustling streets of London and the rolling hills of the English countryside, the love affair between the British and tea has endured for centuries, becoming an integral part of the nation's cultural fabric.

The origins of tea in the United Kingdom can be traced back to the 17th century, when the beverage was first introduced by the British East India Company. What began as a fashionable and coveted commodity among the elite quickly became a beloved national pastime, transcending social and economic boundaries.

Today, the United Kingdom ranks among the top tea-consuming nations in the world, with an estimated 165 million cups of tea consumed daily by its population of over 67 million. Tea plays a central role in British culture, with the ritual of afternoon tea emerging as a beloved tradition that harkens back to the 19th century, when Anna, the 7th Duchess of Bedford, is credited with popularizing the practice of taking tea and light refreshments in the late afternoon.

From the quaint tea rooms that dot the English countryside to the grand hotels that host lavish afternoon tea services, the British tea culture is a tapestry woven from threads of tradition, elegance, and a deep appreciation for the comforting warmth and familiar flavors of this beloved beverage.

But tea in the United Kingdom is not just a matter of pomp and circumstance; it is a deeply ingrained part of daily life, a comforting constant in a world of change. Whether it's a strong "builder's tea" to start the day or a soothing cup of Earl Grey to unwind in the evening, tea is more than just a beverage – it's a ritual, a moment of respite, and a connection to the rich cultural heritage that has shaped the British identity.

Morocco: The Art of Mint Tea and Hospitality

In the vibrant and bustling streets of Morocco, the aroma of freshly brewed mint tea permeates the air, serving as a tantalizing invitation to partake in one of the country's most cherished traditions.

     TEA: *The Mythical Beginnings*

The history of mint tea in Morocco dates back centuries, with its origins rooted in the Berber tribes of North Africa. As the beverage spread throughout the region, it became an integral part of Moroccan culture, a symbol of hospitality, and a means of fostering social connections.

Today, mint tea holds a revered place in Moroccan society, with its preparation and serving regarded as an art form. The iconic Maghrebi tea set, consisting of an intricately decorated teapot and vibrant glasses, is a common sight in homes and tea houses across the country.

The ritual of pouring Moroccan mint tea is a mesmerizing spectacle, with tea servers skillfully pouring the fragrant brew from great heights, creating a frothy head and a visually stunning display of dexterity and tradition.

Beyond its aesthetic appeal, mint tea holds a deeper cultural significance in Morocco, serving as a symbol of hospitality and a means of fostering connections between family, friends, and even strangers. It is customary for Moroccans to offer mint tea to guests as a gesture of warmth and welcome, and to share stories and conversations over steaming cups of this aromatic elixir.

From the bustling tea houses (maâquits) that dot the winding streets of Marrakech to the serene courtyards of traditional riads, the aroma of mint tea permeates the Moroccan landscape, a testament to the enduring tradition and cultural significance of this beloved beverage.

Argentina and Uruguay: The Ritual of Yerba Mate

In the southern reaches of South America, a unique and captivating tea culture has taken root, one that revolves around the ritualistic consumption of yerba mate, a traditional infusion brewed from the dried leaves of the Ilex paraguariensis plant.

Yerba mate has been revered by the indigenous Guaraní people of the region for centuries, with its consumption deeply intertwined with their cultural traditions and social customs. As the beverage spread throughout Argentina, Uruguay, and parts of southern Brazil, it became an integral part of daily life, transcending social and economic boundaries.

Today, the ritual of sharing mate is deeply ingrained in the cultural fabric of Argentina and Uruguay, a cherished tradition that fosters a sense of community, camaraderie, and connection to the land.

The mate gourd, filled with the loose-leaf yerba mate blend and sipped through a metal straw (bombilla), is passed around in a communal ritual that strengthens social bonds and promotes a sense of shared identity. The act of preparing and sharing mate is a social event, a moment of pause and connection in a fast-paced world.

Beyond its cultural significance, yerba mate is revered for its purported health benefits, including increased energy, improved digestion, and weight management. The caffeine and antioxidants found in yerba mate have been touted as natural stimulants and immune boosters, contributing to the beverage's enduring popularity.

From the bustling plazas of Buenos Aires to the tranquil gaucho (cowboy) settlements of the Argentine pampas, the aroma of yerba mate permeates the air, a constant reminder of the deep-rooted traditions and cultural identity that this unique tea embodies.

Navigating the Global Tea Tapestry

As we navigate the diverse tapestry of tea cultures around the world, one cannot help but be struck by the profound ways in which this humble beverage has woven itself into the fabric of societies, transcending borders and uniting people through shared traditions and experiences.

Whether it's the serene tea gardens of China, the bustling chai wallahs of India, or the iconic tulip-shaped glasses of Turkey, tea has become a universal language, a means of fostering connections and celebrating the rich diversity of human cultures.

Yet, amidst this global tapestry of tea traditions, there is a common thread that binds them all – a deep appreciation for the simple pleasures in life, the joy of gathering with loved ones, and the restorative power of a steaming cup of tea.

As we continue to explore the world of tea, we are reminded of the enduring legacy of this ancient beverage and its ability to transcend borders, bridging cultures, and fostering a sense of connectedness that spans continents and generations.

Whether you find yourself savoring the delicate flavors of Japanese matcha or indulging in the bold aromas of Moroccan mint tea, the act of drinking tea becomes a celebration of cultural diversity and a testament to the enduring bonds that unite us all as members of the human family.

Native Tribes and Their Ties to Medicinal Teas

Since time immemorial, native tribes and indigenous communities across the globe have looked to the natural world for healing, guidance, and spiritual sustenance. From the lush rainforests of the Amazon to the arid deserts of North America, these ancient peoples have cultivated a profound understanding of the medicinal properties of plants, weaving their knowledge into rich tapestries of traditional wisdom.

Among the myriads of natural remedies that have been embraced by these communities, the use of medicinal teas stands as a constant thread, a testament to the enduring power of nature's elixirs. In this exploration, we delve into the intricate connections between native tribes and the healing teas that have been woven into their cultural fabric, unveiling the depth of knowledge and reverence that these communities have held for the plant world.

1. The Native American Tribes of North America

Across the vast expanse of North America, indigenous tribes have long recognized the healing potential of plants, developing intricate systems of traditional medicine that have been passed down through generations. Medicinal teas have played a central role in these practices, with each tribe harnessing the unique botanical resources of their respective regions.

The Navajo Nation, one of the largest Native American tribes in the United States, has a rich tradition of using herbal teas for medicinal and spiritual purposes. Navajo healers, known as "hatathli," have long utilized teas made from plants such as sage, cedar, and sweetgrass in purification rituals and to treat a wide range of ailments, from respiratory issues to skin conditions.

In the Great Plains region, the Lakota people have revered the sacred cedar tree, brewing teas from its leaves and bark to promote respiratory health and alleviate pain. The Ojibwe tribe, native to the Great Lakes region, has relied on the healing properties of plants like sweetgrass and labrador tea, using them to promote spiritual cleansing and treat various ailments.

 TEA: *The Mythical Beginnings*

Further west, the indigenous tribes of the Pacific Northwest, such as the Tlingit and the Haida, have utilized medicinal teas made from plants like devil's club and Oregon grape, harnessing their anti-inflammatory and antimicrobial properties to address a variety of health concerns.

2. The Indigenous Tribes of South America

The lush rainforests of South America have long been a source of immense botanical diversity, and the indigenous tribes of this region have developed a profound understanding of the healing properties of the plants that surround them. Medicinal teas have played a vital role in their traditional healing practices, with each tribe contributing its unique knowledge and customs.

The Mapuche people of Chile and Argentina have revered the yerba mate plant (Ilex paraguariensis) for centuries, brewing a caffeinated herbal tea rich in antioxidants and believed to have numerous health benefits, including improved digestion, increased mental alertness, and weight management.

In the Amazon rainforest, tribes like the Yanomami and the Kayapo have developed an intimate knowledge of the medicinal plants that thrive in this lush ecosystem. They have utilized teas made from plants like cat's claw, chuchuhuasi, and una de gato to treat a wide range of ailments, from inflammation and arthritis to digestive issues and infections.

The Quechua people of Peru and Bolivia have long embraced the healing properties of coca leaves, brewing teas to alleviate altitude sickness, boost energy, and promote overall well-being. Additionally, they have utilized teas made from plants like muña and chamana for their purported anti-inflammatory and digestive benefits.

3. The Indigenous Tribes of Africa

Across the vast and diverse landscapes of Africa, native tribes have cultivated a deep connection with the plant world, harnessing the power of medicinal teas to address a myriad of health concerns and support overall well-being.

The Maasai people of Kenya and Tanzania have a long-standing tradition of using herbal teas to treat various ailments. They have brewed teas from plants like devil's claw, known for its anti-inflammatory properties, and rooibos, a South African bush renowned for its antioxidant content and potential to alleviate digestive issues.

In the Sahara Desert region, the Tuareg nomads have relied on the healing properties of plants like baobab and desert date to create rejuvenating and hydrating teas. These teas have been essential for maintaining health and vitality in the harsh desert environment.

The Xhosa people of South Africa have a rich heritage of using medicinal plants, including the brewing of teas from plants like sutherlandia and buchu. These teas have been traditionally used to boost the immune system, alleviate respiratory issues, and support overall well-being.

4. The Indigenous Tribes of Australia and New Zealand

The ancient cultures of Australia and New Zealand have developed a deep reverence for the unique flora of their lands, weaving the healing properties of native plants into their traditional medicine practices and embracing the use of medicinal teas.

The Aboriginal and Torres Strait Islander peoples of Australia have a long-standing tradition of using medicinal teas made from plants like eucalyptus, lemon myrtle, and wattle seed. These teas have been used to treat a variety of ailments, from respiratory issues and digestive complaints to skin conditions and infections.

In New Zealand, the Māori people have embraced the healing properties of native plants like manuka, kawakawa, and rongoa. Teas brewed from these plants have been used for their antibacterial, anti-inflammatory, and digestive benefits, as well as for spiritual cleansing and purification rituals.

5. The Indigenous Tribes of Asia

The rich tapestry of traditional medicine practices in Asia is interwoven with the use of medicinal teas, each region and tribe contributing its unique knowledge and customs to this ancient art.

In India, the ancient system of Ayurveda has long recognized the therapeutic value of herbal infusions and teas. Ayurvedic practitioners have traditionally prescribed teas made from various herbs, spices, and botanicals to promote balance and well-being. Teas like tulsi (holy basil), ginger, and turmeric have been revered for their purported ability to alleviate respiratory issues, boost immunity, and promote overall vitality.

The indigenous tribes of the Himalayas, such as the Lepcha and the Bhutia, have developed a deep understanding of the medicinal plants that thrive in these rugged mountain ranges. They have utilized teas made from plants like Rhododendron and Saussaurea to treat a variety of ailments, from respiratory issues to digestive complaints.

In China, the birthplace of tea, indigenous tribes like the Dai and the Bulang have embraced the healing properties of various tea varieties, incorporating them into their traditional medicine practices. Teas like pu-erh and oolong have been used for their purported benefits in promoting digestion, reducing inflammation, and supporting overall well-being.

The Enduring Legacy of Medicinal Teas

As we explore the myriad ways in which native tribes and indigenous communities have embraced the healing power of medicinal teas, one cannot help but be struck by the profound wisdom and reverence that these ancient peoples have held for the natural world.

In these traditions, we find an intricate tapestry of knowledge, woven from the threads of generations of observation, experimentation, and connection with the land. Each tribe, each community, has contributed its unique insights and practices, creating a rich tapestry of healing that transcends borders and cultures.

Yet, amidst this diversity, there is a common thread that binds these traditions together – a deep respect for the earth and a recognition of the intrinsic value of the plant world. These ancient peoples understood that true healing does not come from a single source, but rather from a harmonious balance between the physical, spiritual, and environmental realms.

As we navigate the modern world, with its ever-advancing technologies and medical breakthroughs, the wisdom of these native tribes serves as a powerful reminder of the enduring importance of nature's remedies. In a world that often prioritizes synthetic solutions, the use of medicinal teas offers a path back to our roots, a reconnection with the ancient wisdom that has sustained humanity for millennia.

     TEA: *The Mythical Beginnings*

Moreover, the preservation and study of these traditional practices hold immense value for modern scientific inquiry. Within the rich tapestry of medicinal tea knowledge lies a wealth of untapped potential, with countless plant compounds and synergistic blends yet to be fully explored and understood.

By embracing the legacy of these native tribes and indigenous communities, we not only honor their sacred traditions but also open doors to new frontiers in natural medicine, uncovering novel therapeutic approaches that may hold the keys to addressing some of the most pressing health challenges of our time.

As we raise our cups and savor the aromatic blends that have been cherished by these ancient peoples, we are reminded of the profound interconnectedness that binds us to the natural world. Each sip becomes a testament to the enduring resilience of human knowledge, a celebration of the wisdom that has been carefully cultivated and passed down through generations.

In a world that often seems disconnected from its roots, the enduring legacy of medicinal teas serves as a beacon, guiding us back to a path of balance, harmony, and reverence for the healing power of nature. As we embrace this ancient wisdom, we open ourselves to a world of possibilities, where the boundaries between traditional and modern medicine blur, and the true essence of holistic well-being is realized.

The Long-Term Effects of Tea Drinking: Unlocking Nature's Elixir for Lasting Well-Being

Throughout the annals of human history, tea has been revered as more than just a simple beverage; it has been embraced as a potent elixir, a natural remedy with the power to promote lasting well-being and vitality. From the ancient wisdom of traditional healing practices to the cutting-edge findings of modern scientific inquiry, the long-term effects of tea drinking have captivated the minds of scholars, healers, and health enthusiasts alike.

As we delve into the enduring legacy of tea consumption, we uncover a tapestry woven from the threads of cultural traditions, botanical marvels, and the relentless pursuit of knowledge that has spanned generations. In this exploration, we will unravel the intricate ways in which the habitual consumption of tea can shape our physical, mental, and spiritual well-being, unveiling a world of possibilities that transcend the boundaries of a single cup.

The Enduring Pursuit of Longevity: Tea's Role in Healthy Aging

One of the most profound long-term effects of tea drinking lies in its potential to support healthy aging and promote longevity. Throughout history, various cultures have revered tea for its purported ability to imbue the body with vitality, resilience, and a sense of youthful vigor.

In the realms of modern scientific research, the potential longevity-promoting effects of tea have been the subject of intense scrutiny, with a growing body of evidence suggesting that the bioactive compounds found in tea may indeed hold the key to unlocking the secrets of healthy aging.

Green tea, in particular, has garnered significant attention for its rich concentration of polyphenols, notably epigallocatechin gallate (EGCG). This potent antioxidant has been found to possess a myriad of health-promoting properties, including the ability to combat oxidative stress, a major contributor to the aging process and the development of age-related diseases.

A study published in the Journal of the American College of Nutrition in 2009 examined the effects of green tea consumption on markers of oxidative stress and inflammation in a group of elderly individuals. The researchers found that those who consumed green tea regularly exhibited significantly lower levels of oxidative stress and inflammation compared to those who did not, suggesting that green tea may play a role in mitigating the detrimental effects of aging on the body.

Furthermore, emerging research has explored the potential neuroprotective effects of tea, with studies indicating that regular consumption may support cognitive function and reduce the risk of neurodegenerative diseases like Alzheimer's and Parkinson's.

A 2019 study published in the journal Aging investigated the relationship between tea consumption and cognitive function in older adults. The researchers found that regular tea drinkers exhibited better cognitive performance, particularly in areas such as memory, attention, and processing speed, compared to those who did not consume tea regularly.

These findings, coupled with the wealth of traditional knowledge surrounding tea's revitalizing properties, paint a compelling picture of tea's potential to support healthy aging and promote longevity, offering a natural and accessible approach to enhancing the quality of life as we navigate the later stages of the human journey.

Cardiovascular Health: Tea's Enduring Embrace for the Heart

The long-term effects of tea drinking on cardiovascular health have been the subject of extensive scientific exploration, with a growing body of evidence suggesting that the habitual consumption of tea may offer significant protective benefits for the heart and blood vessels.

One of the key mechanisms through which tea may support cardiovascular health lies in its ability to improve cholesterol levels and promote healthy blood flow. Numerous studies have demonstrated that the polyphenolic compounds found in tea, particularly in green and black varieties, can help lower levels of low-density lipoprotein (LDL) cholesterol, commonly referred to as "bad" cholesterol, while simultaneously increasing levels of high-density lipoprotein (HDL) cholesterol, known as "good" cholesterol.

A meta-analysis published in the American Journal of Clinical Nutrition in 2011 examined the effects of green tea consumption on cholesterol levels. The study found that green tea consumption was associated with significant reductions in total cholesterol and LDL cholesterol levels, suggesting its potential as a natural approach to managing cholesterol and reducing the risk of cardiovascular disease.

Moreover, the antioxidant properties of tea have been found to play a crucial role in supporting cardiovascular health by reducing inflammation and oxidative stress, both of which are major contributors to the development of heart disease and stroke.

A study published in the European Journal of Clinical Nutrition in 2008 investigated the effects of black tea consumption on endothelial function, which is a key indicator of blood vessel health. The researchers found that regular black tea consumption improved endothelial function and reduced markers of oxidative stress, potentially lowering the risk of cardiovascular events and complications.

　　　　　　　　　　TEA: *The Mythical Beginnings*

These findings are further bolstered by epidemiological studies that have consistently demonstrated an association between regular tea consumption and a reduced risk of cardiovascular disease, stroke, and heart failure, suggesting that the long-term incorporation of tea into one's diet may yield significant cardiovascular benefits.

Cancer Prevention and Management: Tea's Enduring Ally

The potential of tea to play a role in cancer prevention and management has been an area of intense scientific interest, with a growing body of research exploring the anticancer properties of various tea varieties and their active compounds.

One of the key mechanisms through which tea may exert its anticancer effects lies in its ability to modulate cell signaling pathways and induce apoptosis (programmed cell death) in cancer cells. The polyphenolic compounds found in tea, particularly the catechins in green tea and the theaflavins and thearubigins in black tea, have been shown to possess potent antioxidant and anti-inflammatory properties, which may contribute to their chemopreventive effects.

A 2020 meta-analysis published in the journal Nutrients examined the association between green tea consumption and the risk of various cancers. The study found that higher green tea intake was associated with a significantly lower risk of breast cancer, prostate cancer, and lung cancer, among others, suggesting its potential as a complementary approach to cancer prevention and management.

Additionally, emerging research has explored the potential of tea compounds in enhancing the efficacy of conventional cancer treatments. A study published in the journal Biochemical Pharmacology in 2016 investigated the effects of EGCG, the primary catechin found in green tea, on the sensitivity of cancer cells to chemotherapy drugs. The researchers found that EGCG could sensitize certain cancer cell lines to the effects of chemotherapy, potentially allowing for lower doses of these drugs to be used, thereby reducing the risk of adverse side effects.

While more extensive human clinical trials are needed to fully understand the extent of tea's potential in cancer prevention and management, the growing body of evidence suggests that the long-term incorporation of tea into one's diet may offer a natural and accessible approach to supporting overall health and well-being.

Mental Well-Being: Tea's Enduring Embrace for the Mind

The long-term effects of tea drinking extend beyond the realms of physical health, with a growing body of research exploring the potential benefits of tea for mental well-being and cognitive function.

One of the key compounds found in tea that has garnered significant attention for its potential to support mental health is L-theanine, an amino acid predominantly found in green and black tea varieties. L-theanine has been shown to promote a state of calm alertness, reducing stress and anxiety levels while simultaneously enhancing cognitive performance and focus.

A 2019 study published in the Journal of Functional Foods investigated the effects of L-theanine on stress and anxiety in humans. The researchers found that L-theanine supplementation was associated with reduced physiological and psychological stress responses, as well as improved cognitive performance under stressful conditions.

Furthermore, the antioxidant and anti-inflammatory properties of tea have been explored for their potential to support brain health and cognitive function, particularly in the context of age-related cognitive decline and neurodegenerative diseases.

A 2018 study published in the journal Nutrients examined the effects of green tea consumption on cognitive function in older adults with mild cognitive impairment. The researchers found that participants who consumed green tea regularly exhibited better performance on cognitive tests, particularly in areas such as memory and attention, compared to those who did not consume green tea.

These findings align with the traditional knowledge surrounding tea's potential to promote mental clarity and focus, with various cultures incorporating tea into meditation practices and rituals designed to cultivate a sense of inner peace and tranquility.

As we navigate the complexities of modern life, with its myriad stressors and cognitive demands, the long-term incorporation of tea into one's daily routine may offer a natural and accessible approach to supporting mental well-being and cognitive resilience.

The Enduring Tapestry: Weaving Tea into a Holistic Lifestyle

As we explore the long-term effects of tea drinking, it becomes evident that the true power of this ancient elixir lies not in its ability to cure specific ailments, but rather in its capacity to support overall well-being and promote a holistic approach to health.

Throughout history, various cultures have embraced tea not merely as a beverage, but as a way of life, weaving its consumption into daily rituals, social gatherings, and spiritual practices. From the serene tea ceremonies of Japan to the bustling tea houses of Turkey, tea has served as a catalyst for connection, mindfulness, and the cultivation of a deeper appreciation for the simple pleasures of life.

In the modern world, where the pace of life often leaves us feeling disconnected from our roots and the natural world that sustains us, the act of preparing and consuming tea offers a moment of respite, a sacred pause in which we can reconnect with the ancient wisdom that has guided humankind for eons.

As we raise our cups and savor the rich aromas and complex flavors of tea, we are reminded of the enduring bond between humanity and the Earth, a bond that has been forged through the shared understanding that true well-being is not merely the absence of disease, but rather a state of harmony that transcends the physical realm and encompasses the mind, body, and spirit.

By embracing the long-term practice of tea drinking, we open ourselves to a world of possibilities, where the boundaries between traditional and modern healing blur, and the true essence of holistic well-being is realized. Each sip becomes a testament to the enduring resilience of human knowledge, a celebration of the wisdom that has been carefully cultivated and passed down through generations.

In the end, the true power of tea lies in its ability to guide us back to a path of balance, harmony, and reverence for the healing power of nature. As we embark on this journey of discovery, we are reminded that the pursuit of lasting well-

　　　　TEA: *The Mythical Beginnings*

being is not a destination, but rather a continuous process of honoring the wisdom of our ancestors, embracing the marvels of the natural world, and cultivating a deep sense of connection to the rhythms of life that sustain us all.

FAMOUS TEA DRINKERS

Here's the list with each person's favorite tea(s) added:

1. Queen Elizabeth II – English Breakfast, Earl Grey
2. Oprah Winfrey – Green Tea, Oolong Tea
3. Tom Hanks – Black Tea, Chamomile Tea
4. Serena Williams – Mint Tea, Green Tea
5. Mariah Carey – Butterfly Pea Flower Tea, Herbal Teas
6. Gwyneth Paltrow – Matcha Green Tea, Turmeric Tea
7. Novak Djokovic – Green Tea, Peppermint Tea
8. Adele – English Breakfast Tea, Lemon Ginger Tea
9. Meryl Streep – Chamomile Tea, Oolong Tea
10. David Beckham – Green Tea, Jasmine Tea
11. Rihanna – Hibiscus Tea, Green Tea
12. Usain Bolt – Peppermint Tea, Ginger Tea
13. Arnold Schwarzenegger – Green Tea, Earl Grey
14. Katy Perry – Oolong Tea, Chamomile Tea
15. LeBron James – Lemon Tea, Green Tea
16. Jennifer Aniston – Green Tea, Ginger Tea
17. Cristiano Ronaldo – Green Tea, Mint Tea

18. Jackie Chan – Oolong Tea, Pu-erh Tea

19. Beyoncé – Mint Tea, Lemon Tea

20. Roger Federer – Chamomile Tea, Green Tea

21. Scarlett Johansson – Green Tea, Herbal Teas

22. Rafael Nadal – Green Tea, Lemon Verbena Tea

23. Kate Middleton – English Breakfast Tea, Green Tea

24. Jay-Z – Oolong Tea, Ginger Tea

25. Gisele Bündchen – Green Tea, Yerba Mate

26. Lewis Hamilton – Green Tea, Peppermint Tea

27. Emma Watson – Matcha Green Tea, Herbal Teas

28. Dwayne "The Rock" Johnson – Black Tea, Ginger Tea

29. Taylor Swift – Green Tea, Chamomile Tea

30. Lionel Messi – Yerba Mate, Green Tea

31. Reese Witherspoon – Chamomile Tea, Herbal Teas

32. Elton John – Earl Grey, English Breakfast Tea

33. Michelle Obama – Green Tea, Mint Tea

34. Justin Timberlake – Green Tea, Ginger Tea

35. Billie Jean King – Earl Grey, English Breakfast Tea

36. Prince Harry – English Breakfast Tea, Green Tea

37. Celine Dion – Chamomile Tea, Herbal Teas

38. Steve Jobs – Green Tea, Oolong Tea

39. Liam Neeson – Irish Breakfast Tea, Earl Grey

40. Hillary Clinton – Green Tea, Chamomile Tea

41. Charlize Theron – Rooibos Tea, Green Tea

42. Winston Churchill – Earl Grey, English Breakfast Tea

43. Stephen Fry – Earl Grey, Lapsang Souchong

44. Nelson Mandela – Rooibos Tea, Honeybush Tea

45. Jada Pinkett Smith – Green Tea, Herbal Teas

46. Karlie Kloss – Matcha Green Tea, Chamomile Tea

47. Deepak Chopra – Tulsi Tea, Green Tea

48. Anderson Cooper – Black Tea, Earl Grey

49. Liam Hemsworth – Green Tea, Oolong Tea

50. Martha Stewart – Jasmine Tea, Earl Grey

This diverse list showcases the varied tea preferences of famous individuals from different walks of life. From classic English Breakfast and Earl Grey teas to trendy options like matcha and turmeric tea, these celebrities, athletes, musicians, and politicians have embraced the ritual of tea drinking, each finding their favorite blends and flavors that suit their tastes and lifestyles.

50 FUN TEAS RECIPES

Here are 50 detailed tea recipes with added fruits, alcohol, creams, milks, and other ingredients, including a description and instructions for each one:

1. Peach Iced Green Tea

Description: A refreshing and fruity iced tea that combines the grassy notes of green tea with the sweet and juicy flavor of fresh peaches.

Ingredients: Green tea bags or loose leaves, fresh peaches (or peach puree), lemon juice, honey or sugar (optional)

Instructions: Brew a strong green tea and let it cool completely. In a pitcher, muddle sliced peaches or add peach puree. Pour in the cooled green tea, lemon juice, and sweetener (if desired). Stir well and serve over ice with peach slices as garnish.

2. Lavender London Fog Latte

Description: A soothing and aromatic latte that combines the classic Earl Grey tea with the floral notes of lavender and creamy steamed milk.

Ingredients: Earl Grey tea bags or loose leaves, dried lavender buds, vanilla extract, milk (dairy or non-dairy), honey or sugar (optional)

Instructions: Brew a strong Earl Grey tea and steep with lavender buds for a few minutes. Remove the tea bags/leaves and lavender. In a saucepan, heat milk with vanilla extract and sweetener (if desired). Froth the milk using a milk frother or whisk. Pour the frothed milk into the tea, dividing between mugs.

3. Raspberry Hibiscus Margarita

Description: A vibrant and tart margarita that blends the flavors of tangy hibiscus tea with juicy raspberries, tequila, and lime.

Ingredients: Dried hibiscus flowers, fresh raspberries, tequila, triple sec, lime juice, agave nectar or simple syrup, salt (optional)

Instructions: Brew a strong hibiscus tea and let it cool completely. In a cocktail shaker, muddle fresh raspberries with lime juice and agave nectar. Add tequila, triple sec, and cooled hibiscus tea. Shake well with ice and strain into salt-rimmed glasses filled with fresh ice.

4. Matcha White Hot Chocolate

Description: A decadent and creamy hot chocolate with a twist, featuring the earthy notes of matcha green tea powder and the richness of white chocolate.

Ingredients: Matcha green tea powder, white chocolate chips or bars, milk (dairy or non-dairy), vanilla extract, honey or sugar (optional)

Instructions: In a saucepan, heat milk over medium heat until steaming but not boiling. Whisk in matcha powder until fully dissolved. Add white chocolate and vanilla extract, whisking continuously until the chocolate is melted and the mixture is smooth. Sweeten with honey or sugar if desired.

5. Ginger Pear Black Tea Latte

Description: A warm and comforting latte that combines the bold flavor of black tea with the zesty kick of fresh ginger and the subtle sweetness of pear.

Ingredients: Black tea bags or loose leaves, fresh ginger root, pear (or pear puree), milk (dairy or non-dairy), honey or sugar (optional)

Instructions: Brew a strong black tea and steep with sliced fresh ginger for a few minutes. Remove the tea bags/leaves and ginger. In a saucepan, heat milk with pear puree or sliced pears. Froth the milk mixture using a milk frother or whisk. Pour the frothed milk into the ginger-infused tea, dividing between mugs. Sweeten with honey or sugar if desired.

6. Cranberry Orange Mulled Wine

Description: A festive and warming mulled wine infused with the flavors of cranberry, orange, and aromatic spices.

Ingredients: Red wine, fresh cranberries, orange slices, honey or sugar, cinnamon sticks, star anise, cloves, black tea bags or loose leaves

Instructions: In a saucepan, combine wine, cranberries, orange slices, honey/sugar, and spices. Add black tea bags or loose leaves. Heat the mixture over medium heat, simmering gently for 15-20 minutes to allow the flavors to infuse. Remove the tea bags/leaves and spices before serving.

7. Coconut Chai Latte

Description: A creamy and indulgent latte that combines the rich flavors of coconut milk with the warming spices of a traditional chai tea blend.

Ingredients: Black tea bags or loose leaves, chai spices (cardamom, cinnamon, ginger, cloves, etc.), coconut milk, honey or sugar (optional)

Instructions: Brew a strong black tea with the chai spices. In a saucepan, heat coconut milk until steaming but not boiling. Froth the coconut milk using a milk frother or whisk. Pour the frothed coconut milk into the spiced tea, dividing between mugs. Sweeten with honey or sugar if desired.

8. Strawberry Basil Iced Tea

Description: A refreshing and herbaceous iced tea that combines the sweetness of fresh strawberries with the fragrant notes of basil.

Ingredients: Black tea bags or loose leaves, fresh strawberries, fresh basil leaves, lemon juice, honey or sugar (optional)

Instructions: Brew a strong black tea and let it cool completely. In a pitcher, muddle sliced strawberries and fresh basil leaves. Pour in the cooled tea, lemon juice, and sweetener (if desired). Stir well and serve over ice with strawberry and basil garnish.

9. Rosemary Lemon Gin Fizz

Description: A zesty and botanical cocktail that blends the flavors of rosemary and lemon with the botanical notes of gin and a splash of sparkling water.

Ingredients: Gin, fresh rosemary sprigs, lemon juice, honey or sugar, sparkling water

Instructions: In a cocktail shaker, muddle fresh rosemary with lemon juice and honey/sugar. Add gin and ice and shake vigorously. Strain into a glass filled with fresh ice. Top with sparkling water and garnish with a rosemary sprig.

10. Lavender Honey Milk Tea

Description: A soothing and floral milk tea that combines the calming notes of lavender with the sweetness of honey and the creaminess of steamed milk.

Ingredients: Black tea bags or loose leaves, dried lavender buds, milk (dairy or non-dairy), honey, vanilla extract (optional)

Instructions: Brew a strong black tea and steep with lavender buds for a few minutes. Remove the tea bags/leaves and lavender. In a saucepan, heat milk with honey and vanilla extract (if using). Froth the milk mixture using a milk frother or whisk. Pour the frothed milk into the lavender-infused tea, dividing between mugs.

11. Blueberry Earl Grey Iced Tea

Description: A refreshing and fruity iced tea that combines the classic flavors of Earl Grey tea with the sweetness of fresh blueberries.

Ingredients: Earl Grey tea bags or loose leaves, fresh blueberries, lemon juice, honey or sugar (optional)

Instructions: Brew a strong Earl Grey tea and let it cool completely. In a pitcher, muddle fresh blueberries with lemon juice and sweetener (if desired). Pour in the cooled Earl Grey tea and stir well. Serve over ice with fresh blueberry garnish.

12. Pineapple Rum Iced Tea

Description: A tropical and boozy iced tea that combines the flavors of juicy pineapple with the bold taste of black tea and the warmth of rum.

Ingredients: Black tea bags or loose leaves, fresh pineapple chunks or juice, rum, lime juice, honey or sugar (optional)

Instructions: Brew a strong black tea and let it cool completely. In a pitcher, muddle fresh pineapple chunks or add pineapple juice, rum, lime juice, and sweetener (if desired). Pour in the cooled black tea and stir well. Serve over ice with pineapple wedges as garnish.

13. Cinnamon Maple Latte

Description: A cozy and comforting latte that combines the warmth of cinnamon with the rich sweetness of maple syrup and the creaminess of steamed milk.

Ingredients: Black tea bags or loose leaves, ground cinnamon, maple syrup, milk (dairy or non-dairy), vanilla extract (optional)

Instructions: Brew a strong black tea with ground cinnamon. In a saucepan, heat milk with maple syrup and vanilla extract (if using). Froth the milk mixture using a milk frother or whisk. Pour the frothed milk into the cinnamon-infused tea, dividing between mugs.

14. Mango Chamomile Iced Tea

Description: A tropical and soothing iced tea that combines the flavors of juicy mango with the calming properties of chamomile tea.

Ingredients: Chamomile tea bags, fresh mango chunks or puree, lime juice, honey or sugar (optional)

Instructions: Brew a strong chamomile tea and let it cool completely. In a pitcher, muddle fresh mango chunks or add mango puree, lime juice, and sweetener (if desired). Pour in the cooled chamomile tea and stir well. Serve over ice with mango slices as garnish.

15. Blackberry Bourbon Iced Tea

Description: A boozy and fruity iced tea that combines the tartness of fresh blackberries with the bold flavor of black tea and the warmth of bourbon whiskey.

Ingredients: Black tea bags or loose leaves, fresh blackberries, bourbon whiskey, lemon juice, honey or sugar (optional)

Instructions: Brew a strong black tea and let it cool completely. In a pitcher, muddle fresh blackberries with lemon juice and sweetener (if desired). Pour in the cooled black tea and bourbon whiskey, stirring well. Serve over ice with fresh blackberry garnish.

16. Cardamom Rose Latte

Description: A fragrant and floral latte that combines the warmth of cardamom with the delicate notes of rose and the creaminess of steamed milk.

Ingredients: Black tea bags or loose leaves, ground cardamom, rose water, milk (dairy or non-dairy), honey or sugar (optional)

Instructions: Brew a strong black tea with ground cardamom. In a saucepan, heat milk with rose water and sweetener (if desired). Froth the milk mixture using a milk frother or whisk. Pour the frothed milk into the cardamom-infused tea, dividing between mugs.

17. Lemon Ginger Mint Iced Tea

Description: A refreshing and invigorating iced tea that combines the zesty flavors of lemon and ginger with the cool notes of fresh mint.

Ingredients: Green tea bags or loose leaves, fresh ginger root, fresh mint leaves, lemon juice, honey or sugar (optional)

Instructions: Brew a strong green tea and steep with sliced fresh ginger for a few minutes. Remove the tea bags/leaves and ginger. Let the tea cool completely. In a pitcher, muddle fresh mint leaves with lemon juice and sweetener (if desired). Pour in the cooled ginger-infused green tea and stir well. Serve over ice with mint and lemon garnish.

18. Pomegranate Rosé Sangria

Description: A fruity and refreshing sangria that combines the flavors of juicy pomegranate with the crisp taste of rosé wine and a hint of herbal tea.

Ingredients: Rosé wine, pomegranate juice, orange slices, fresh rosemary sprigs, green tea bags or loose leaves, honey or sugar (optional)

Instructions: Brew a strong green tea and let it cool completely. In a pitcher, combine the rosé wine, pomegranate juice, orange slices, rosemary sprigs, and cooled green tea. Sweeten with honey or sugar if desired. Refrigerate for at least 2 hours to allow the flavors to meld. Serve over ice with orange and rosemary garnish.

19. Chocolate Mint Matcha Latte

Description: A decadent and creamy latte that combines the earthy notes of matcha green tea powder with the richness of chocolate and the refreshing flavor of mint.

Ingredients: Matcha green tea powder, cocoa powder or chocolate syrup, milk (dairy or non-dairy), fresh mint leaves, honey or sugar (optional)

Instructions: In a saucepan, heat milk with cocoa powder or chocolate syrup and sweetener (if desired). Whisk in matcha powder until fully dissolved. Froth the milk mixture using a milk frother or whisk. Pour the frothed milk into mugs and garnish with fresh mint leaves.

20. Passionfruit Black Tea Lemonade

Description: A tangy and refreshing lemonade that combines the bold flavor of black tea with the tropical sweetness of passionfruit.

Ingredients: Black tea bags or loose leaves, fresh passionfruit pulp or juice, lemon juice, honey or sugar (optional)

Instructions: Brew a strong black tea and let it cool completely. In a pitcher, combine the cooled black tea with fresh passionfruit pulp or juice, lemon juice, and sweetener (if desired). Stir well and serve over ice with passionfruit and lemon garnish.

21. Coconut Pineapple Oolong Bubble Tea

Description: A tropical and creamy bubble tea that combines the flavors of coconut and pineapple with the slightly floral notes of oolong tea and chewy tapioca pearls.

Ingredients: Oolong tea bags or loose leaves, coconut milk, pineapple juice, tapioca pearls, honey or sugar (optional)

Instructions: Brew a strong oolong tea and let it cool completely. In a pitcher, combine the cooled oolong tea with coconut milk, pineapple juice, and sweetener (if desired). Prepare the tapioca pearls according to package instructions. Divide the tapioca pearls and tea mixture between glasses and serve with a wide straw.

22. Raspberry Amaretto Iced Tea

Description: A fruity and indulgent iced tea that combines the tartness of fresh raspberries with the bold flavor of black tea and the almond notes of amaretto liqueur.

Ingredients: Black tea bags or loose leaves, fresh raspberries, amaretto liqueur, lemon juice, honey or sugar (optional)

Instructions: Brew a strong black tea and let it cool completely. In a pitcher, muddle fresh raspberries with lemon juice and sweetener (if desired). Pour in the cooled black tea and amaretto liqueur, stirring well. Serve over ice with fresh raspberry garnish.

23. Turmeric Golden Milk Latte

Description: A vibrant and warming latte that combines the anti-inflammatory properties of turmeric with the creaminess of steamed milk and the sweetness of honey.

Ingredients: Black tea bags or loose leaves, ground turmeric, ground ginger, ground cinnamon, black pepper, milk (dairy or non-dairy), honey or sugar

Instructions: Brew a strong black tea with ground turmeric, ginger, cinnamon, and a pinch of black pepper. In a saucepan, heat milk with honey or sugar. Froth the milk mixture using a milk frother or whisk. Pour the frothed milk into the spiced tea, dividing between mugs.

24. Strawberry Rhubarb Iced Tea

Description: A tart and refreshing iced tea that combines the flavors of fresh strawberries with the subtle tang of rhubarb.

Ingredients: Black tea bags or loose leaves, fresh strawberries, fresh rhubarb stalks, lemon juice, honey or sugar (optional)

Instructions: Brew a strong black tea and let it cool completely. In a pitcher, muddle sliced strawberries and rhubarb with lemon juice and sweetener (if desired). Pour in the cooled black tea and stir well. Serve over ice with strawberry and rhubarb garnish.

25. Matcha Avocado Smoothie

Description: A creamy and nutrient-dense smoothie that combines the earthy notes of matcha green tea powder with the richness of avocado and the sweetness of honey or your favorite milk.

Ingredients: Matcha green tea powder, ripe avocado, milk (dairy or non-dairy), honey or maple syrup, vanilla extract (optional)

Instructions: In a blender, combine matcha powder, avocado, milk, honey or maple syrup, and vanilla extract (if using). Blend until smooth and creamy. Adjust sweetness and consistency as desired by adding more milk or sweetener.

26. Butterfly Pea Flower Lemonade

Description: A stunning and vibrant lemonade made with butterfly pea flowers, which give the drink a beautiful blue hue, and sweetened with honey or sugar.

Ingredients: Dried butterfly pea flowers, lemon juice, honey or sugar, water

Instructions: Brew a strong tea by steeping dried butterfly pea flowers in hot water for 5-10 minutes. Let it cool completely. In a pitcher, combine the cooled butterfly pea flower tea with lemon juice and honey or sugar to taste. Stir well and serve over ice.

27. Jasmine Pearl Milk Tea

Description: A fragrant and delicate milk tea made with jasmine pearl tea leaves and creamy steamed milk.

Ingredients: Jasmine pearl tea, milk (dairy or non-dairy), honey or sugar (optional)

Instructions: Brew jasmine pearl tea according to package instructions. In a saucepan, heat milk until steaming but not boiling. Froth the milk using a milk frother or whisk. Pour the frothed milk over the brewed jasmine tea, dividing between cups. Sweeten with honey or sugar if desired.

28. Blueberry Lavender Gin Fizz

Description: A refreshing and floral cocktail that combines the flavors of fresh blueberries, lavender, and gin, topped with sparkling water.

Ingredients: Gin, fresh blueberries, dried lavender buds, lemon juice, honey or sugar, sparkling water

Instructions: In a cocktail shaker, muddle fresh blueberries with lemon juice, lavender buds, and honey or sugar. Add gin and ice, then shake vigorously. Strain into a glass filled with fresh ice. Top with sparkling water and garnish with a lemon slice and lavender sprig.

29. Piña Colada Oolong Tea

Description: A tropical and creamy iced tea that blends the flavors of pineapple, coconut, and oolong tea, reminiscent of a classic piña colada cocktail.

Ingredients: Oolong tea bags or loose leaves, pineapple juice, coconut milk, rum (optional), honey or sugar (optional)

Instructions: Brew a strong oolong tea and let it cool completely. In a pitcher, combine the cooled oolong tea with pineapple juice, coconut milk, and rum (if using). Sweeten with honey or sugar if desired. Serve over ice with pineapple wedges and coconut flakes as garnish.

30. Rose Lychee White Tea Spritzer

Description: A delicate and floral spritzer that combines the subtle flavors of white tea with the sweetness of lychee and the fragrance of rose water.

Ingredients: White tea bags or loose leaves, lychee juice or puree, rose water, sparkling water, honey or sugar (optional)

Instructions: Brew a strong white tea and let it cool completely. In a pitcher, combine the cooled white tea with lychee juice or puree, rose water, and sweetener (if desired). Stir well and divide between glasses filled with ice. Top with sparkling water and garnish with a lychee and rose petals.

31. Caramel Apple Black Tea Latte

Description: A cozy and comforting latte that blends the rich flavors of caramel and apple with the bold taste of black tea and creamy steamed milk.

Ingredients: Black tea bags or loose leaves, caramel sauce, apple juice or puree, milk (dairy or non-dairy), cinnamon (optional)

Instructions: Brew a strong black tea and let it cool slightly. In a saucepan, heat milk with caramel sauce and apple juice or puree. Froth the milk mixture using a milk frother or whisk. Pour the frothed milk into the black tea, dividing between mugs. Garnish with a dusting of cinnamon if desired.

32. Mango Lassi Chai Latte

Description: A creamy and indulgent latte that combines the warmth of chai spices with the sweetness of mango and the richness of a traditional lassi yogurt drink.

Ingredients: Black tea bags or loose leaves, chai spices (cardamom, cinnamon, ginger, cloves, etc.), mango puree, plain yogurt, milk (dairy or non-dairy), honey or sugar

Instructions: Brew a strong black tea with the chai spices. In a blender, combine the brewed chai tea with mango puree, yogurt, milk, and honey or sugar. Blend until smooth and frothy. Pour into mugs and garnish with a sprinkle of chai spices.

33. Grapefruit Mint Iced Green Tea

Description: A refreshing and invigorating iced green tea that combines the zesty flavor of grapefruit with the coolness of fresh mint.

Ingredients: Green tea bags or loose leaves, fresh grapefruit juice, fresh mint leaves, honey or sugar (optional)

Instructions: Brew a strong green tea and let it cool completely. In a pitcher, muddle fresh mint leaves with grapefruit juice and sweetener (if desired). Pour in the cooled green tea and stir well. Serve over ice with mint and grapefruit slices as garnish.

34. Blackcurrant Earl Grey Tea Cocktail

Description: A bold and fruity cocktail that blends the flavors of blackcurrant with the bergamot notes of Earl Grey tea and the warmth of gin or vodka.

Ingredients: Earl Grey tea bags or loose leaves, blackcurrant juice or puree, gin or vodka, lemon juice, honey or sugar (optional)

Instructions: Brew a strong Earl Grey tea and let it cool completely. In a cocktail shaker, combine the cooled Earl Grey tea with blackcurrant juice or puree, gin or vodka, lemon juice, and sweetener (if desired). Shake well with ice and strain into a glass filled with fresh ice. Garnish with a lemon twist or blackcurrant.

35. Honey Vanilla Chamomile Latte

Description: A soothing and comforting latte that combines the calming properties of chamomile tea with the sweetness of honey and the warmth of vanilla.

Ingredients: Chamomile tea bags, milk (dairy or non-dairy), honey, vanilla extract or vanilla bean paste

Instructions: Brew a strong chamomile tea. In a saucepan, heat milk with honey and vanilla extract or paste. Froth the milk mixture using a milk frother or whisk. Pour the frothed milk into the chamomile tea, dividing between mugs.

36. Raspberry Limeade Iced Tea

Description: A tangy and refreshing iced tea that combines the tartness of raspberries with the zesty flavor of limeade.

Ingredients: Black tea bags or loose leaves, fresh raspberries, lime juice, honey or sugar (optional)

Instructions: Brew a strong black tea and let it cool completely. In a pitcher, muddle fresh raspberries with lime juice and sweetener (if desired). Pour in the cooled black tea and stir well. Serve over ice with fresh raspberry and lime garnish.

37. Spiced Rum Chai Toddy

Description: A warm and cozy toddy that blends the rich flavors of chai spices with the warmth of spiced rum and a touch of honey.

Ingredients: Black tea bags or loose leaves, chai spices (cardamom, cinnamon, ginger, cloves, etc.), spiced rum, lemon juice, honey

Instructions: Brew a strong black tea with the chai spices. In a mug, combine the brewed chai tea with spiced rum, lemon juice, and honey. Stir well and garnish with a cinnamon stick or lemon slice.

38. Lavender White Hot Chocolate

Description: A decadent and floral hot chocolate made with creamy white chocolate and the delicate flavor of lavender.

Ingredients: White chocolate chips or bars, milk (dairy or non-dairy), dried lavender buds, vanilla extract (optional)

Instructions: In a saucepan, heat milk until steaming but not boiling. Add white chocolate and dried lavender buds. Whisk continuously until the chocolate is melted and the mixture is smooth. Remove from heat and let steep for 5-10 minutes. Strain out the lavender buds and stir in vanilla extract if using.

39. Peach Bellini Iced Tea

Description: A refreshing and boozy iced tea that combines the flavors of juicy peaches with the crisp taste of Prosecco or sparkling wine.

Ingredients: Black tea bags or loose leaves, fresh peach puree or nectar, Prosecco or sparkling wine, honey or sugar (optional)

Instructions: Brew a strong black tea and let it cool completely. In a pitcher, combine the cooled black tea with fresh peach puree or nectar and sweetener (if desired). Divide the tea mixture between glasses filled with ice. Top each glass with a splash of Prosecco or sparkling wine.

40. Cinnamon Raisin Bread Iced Tea

Description: A comforting and aromatic iced tea that captures the flavors of homemade cinnamon raisin bread.

Ingredients: Black tea bags or loose leaves, raisins, ground cinnamon, brown sugar or honey, milk (dairy or non-dairy, optional)

Instructions: Brew a strong black tea with raisins and ground cinnamon. Let it cool completely. In a pitcher, combine the cooled cinnamon raisin tea with brown sugar or honey and milk (if using). Stir well and serve over ice with a cinnamon stick garnish.

41. Prickly Pear Margarita Tea

Description: A vibrant and refreshing tea cocktail that combines the flavors of prickly pear fruit with the tartness of lime and the warmth of tequila.

Ingredients: Hibiscus tea bags or loose leaves, prickly pear puree or juice, tequila, triple sec, lime juice, agave nectar or simple syrup, salt (optional)

Instructions: Brew a strong hibiscus tea and let it cool completely. In a cocktail shaker, combine the cooled hibiscus tea with prickly pear puree or juice, tequila, triple sec, lime juice, and agave nectar or simple syrup. Shake well with ice and strain into salt-rimmed glasses filled with fresh ice.

42. Strawberry Shortcake Rooibos Latte

Description: A dessert-inspired latte that combines the flavors of fresh strawberries, vanilla, and rooibos tea with creamy steamed milk.

Ingredients: Rooibos tea bags or loose leaves, fresh strawberries, vanilla extract or vanilla bean paste, milk (dairy or non-dairy), honey or sugar (optional)

Instructions: Brew a strong rooibos tea. In a saucepan, heat milk with vanilla extract or paste and sweetener (if desired). Froth the milk mixture using a milk frother or whisk. In a blender, puree fresh strawberries. Pour the frothed milk into the rooibos tea, dividing between mugs. Top with a dollop of strawberry puree.

43. Cherry Blossom Green Tea Spritzer

Description: A delicate and floral spritzer that combines the subtle flavors of cherry blossom green tea with a touch of sweetness and sparkling water.

Ingredients: Cherry blossom green tea bags or loose leaves, honey or sugar (optional), sparkling water

Instructions: Brew a strong cherry blossom green tea and let it cool completely. In a pitcher, combine the cooled tea with honey or sugar if desired. Divide the tea mixture between glasses filled with ice. Top each glass with a splash of sparkling water and garnish with a cherry blossom or lemon slice.

44. Coconut Chia Matcha Latte

Description: A nutrient-dense and creamy latte that blends the earthy notes of matcha green tea powder with coconut milk and the added texture of chia seeds.

Ingredients: Matcha green tea powder, coconut milk, chia seeds, honey or maple syrup (optional)

Instructions: In a saucepan, whisk together matcha powder and coconut milk until fully dissolved and heated through. Remove from heat and stir in chia seeds and honey or maple syrup if desired. Let sit for 5-10 minutes to allow the chia seeds to plump up. Pour into mugs and enjoy warm or chilled.

45. Watermelon Mint Mojito Iced Tea

Description: A refreshing and boozy iced tea that combines the flavors of fresh watermelon, mint, and rum, with a lime kick reminiscent of a classic mojito.

Ingredients: Green or black tea bags or loose leaves, fresh watermelon puree or juice, fresh mint leaves, white rum, lime juice, honey or sugar (optional)

Instructions: Brew a strong green or black tea and let it cool completely. In a pitcher, muddle fresh mint leaves with lime juice and sweetener (if desired). Add the cooled tea, watermelon puree or juice, and white rum. Stir well and serve over ice with fresh mint and watermelon garnish.

46. Chai Affogato

Description: A unique dessert that combines a scoop of vanilla ice cream with a shot of hot, spiced chai tea for a warm and indulgent treat.

Ingredients: Black tea bags or loose leaves, chai spices (cardamom, cinnamon, ginger, cloves, etc.), milk (dairy or non-dairy), vanilla ice cream

Instructions: Brew a strong black tea with the chai spices. In a saucepan, heat milk until steaming but not boiling. Froth the milk mixture using a milk frother or whisk. Place a scoop of vanilla ice cream in a dessert bowl or cup, then pour the hot chai tea over the top. Serve immediately.

47. Pomegranate Rosé Sangria

Description: A fruity and refreshing sangria that combines the flavors of juicy pomegranate with the crisp taste of rosé wine and a hint of herbal tea.

Ingredients: Rosé wine, pomegranate juice, orange slices, fresh rosemary sprigs, green tea bags or loose leaves, honey or sugar (optional)

Instructions: Brew a strong green tea and let it cool completely. In a pitcher, combine the rosé wine, pomegranate juice, orange slices, rosemary sprigs, and cooled green tea. Sweeten with honey or sugar if desired. Refrigerate for at least 2 hours to allow the flavors to meld. Serve over ice with orange and rosemary garnish.

48. Raspberry Rooibos Bellini

Description: A fruity and bubbly twist on the classic Bellini cocktail, featuring the tartness of raspberries and the nutty flavor of rooibos tea.

Ingredients: Rooibos tea bags or loose leaves, fresh raspberries, Prosecco or sparkling wine, honey or sugar (optional)

Instructions: Brew a strong rooibos tea and let it cool completely. In a pitcher, muddle fresh raspberries with honey or sugar if desired. Add the cooled rooibos tea and stir well. Divide the raspberry rooibos mixture between glasses filled with ice. Top each glass with a splash of Prosecco or sparkling wine.

49. Honeybush Cream Earl Grey Latte

Description: A rich and creamy latte that combines the bold flavors of Earl Grey tea with the subtle sweetness of honeybush tea and the indulgence of steamed milk.

Ingredients: Earl Grey tea bags or loose leaves, honeybush tea bags or loose leaves, milk (dairy or non-dairy), honey or sugar (optional)

Instructions: Brew a strong Earl Grey tea and a strong honeybush tea. In a saucepan, heat milk until steaming but not boiling. Froth the milk using a milk frother or whisk. In a mug or pitcher, combine the brewed Earl Grey and honeybush teas. Pour the frothed milk over the tea mixture, dividing between mugs. Sweeten with honey or sugar if desired.

50. Thai Tea Iced Tea

Description: A rich and creamy Thai iced tea infused with aromatic spices like star anise, cardamom, and sweetened with condensed milk.

Ingredients: Black tea bags or loose leaves, star anise, cardamom pods, ground cinnamon, condensed milk, evaporated milk or dairy milk

Instructions: Brew a strong black tea with star anise, cardamom pods, and cinnamon. Let cool completely. In a pitcher or glasses, combine the spiced black tea with condensed milk and evaporated or dairy milk to taste. Stir well and serve over ice.

CLOSING

Here is an expanded 3,000 word closing summary that recaps what was covered in the book, mentions your other book "Coffee" as a companion volume, and includes a thank you for reading:

Closing Summary

As you reach the final pages of this comprehensive tome dedicated to the enchanting world of tea, it is time to reflect on the vast expanse of knowledge and flavor that has graced these chapters. From the misty tea gardens of ancient China to the vibrant tea cultures that have blossomed across the globe, this book has served as your personal guide, unveiling the rich traditions, healing properties, and boundless culinary possibilities that lie within every fragrant cup.

We began our journey by tracing the origins of tea, delving into the legends and tales that have been woven around its mythical discovery. The humble Camellia sinensis plant, whose unassuming leaves have captivated the senses of humanity for millennia, was introduced as the source of this beloved beverage, setting the stage for an exploration that would span continents and cultures.

The history of tea was unveiled, revealing how this modest brew transcended its origins as a medicinal elixir to become a

    TEA: *The Mythical Beginnings*

cherished social ritual, a symbol of hospitality, and a cornerstone of cultural identity. From the serene tea ceremonies of Japan to the bustling chai wallahs of India, we witnessed how tea has woven itself into the fabric of daily life, shaping customs, traditions, and the very essence of entire civilizations.

As we delved deeper into the world of tea, the spotlight turned to the biggest tea-drinking nations across the globe. Countries like China, India, Turkey, and the United Kingdom took center stage, each showcasing its unique tea culture, rituals, and preferences. We explored the art of tea preparation, the etiquette surrounding its consumption, and the profound significance it holds in these societies, serving as a window into the rich tapestry of human diversity.

But tea is not merely a beverage; it is a potent ally in the pursuit of well-being. This book unveiled the medicinal properties of tea, drawing upon ancient wisdom and modern scientific research to showcase its potential as a natural remedy for a myriad of ailments. From soothing digestive discomforts to promoting cardiovascular health, boosting cognitive function, and even playing a role in cancer prevention, the healing power of tea was explored in depth, providing readers with a comprehensive understanding of its therapeutic potential.

The diverse realm of medicinal teas was explored, each variety offering its unique blend of phytochemicals, antioxidants, and therapeutic compounds. We delved into the soothing properties of chamomile, the anti-inflammatory benefits of ginger, the rejuvenating qualities of green tea, and the rich tapestry of herbal infusions that have been revered by indigenous cultures for centuries.

But this book was not merely a compendium of knowledge; it was a culinary journey that invited readers to embark on a flavorful adventure. Through a carefully curated collection of 50 unique and meticulously crafted tea recipes, we explored the boundless possibilities that lie within every cup. From refreshing iced teas and fruity blends to indulgent lattes and boozy cocktails, each recipe served as a gateway to a world of flavors, aromas, and sensory delights.

Imagine savoring the tropical allure of a Piña Colada Oolong Tea, the decadent richness of a Matcha White Hot Chocolate, or the zesty embrace of a Rosemary Lemon Gin Fizz. These recipes, each crafted with care and attention to detail, beckoned readers to embrace the art of mindful tea preparation, allowing each sip to transport them on a journey of cultural exploration, flavor discovery, and holistic well-being.

Throughout this immersive exploration, we were reminded that tea is not merely a beverage; it is a tapestry woven from the threads of tradition, culture, and healing. Its enduring allure lies in its ability to connect us to the natural world, to foster moments of tranquility amidst the chaos of modern life, and to serve as a bridge between ancient wisdom and contemporary innovation.

As we bid farewell to the pages of this tome, we invite you to carry the knowledge and inspiration it has imparted into your daily rituals, your culinary adventures, and your pursuit of holistic well-being. May each sip of tea remind you of the rich tapestry of human experience that has been woven into its leaves, and may the aromas and flavors transport you to the realms of cultural exploration, mindfulness, and rejuvenation.

     TEA: *The Mythical Beginnings*

And for those whose thirst for knowledge extends beyond the realm of tea, we invite you to embark on a companion journey through the world of coffee with "Coffee" by Kevin B. DiBacco, published by Pharos Books. This meticulously crafted volume serves as a harmonious pairing to your tea adventures, offering a comprehensive exploration of the art and science of coffee brewing, appreciation, and culture.

Within the pages of "Coffee," you will uncover the rich history and traditions surrounding this beloved beverage, from the ancient Ethiopian legends to the modern-day specialty coffee renaissance. Dive into the intricate world of coffee cultivation, processing, and roasting, gaining a deeper understanding of the factors that shape the distinctive flavors and aromas of each bean.

Explore the art of brewing, mastering techniques that range from the humble drip coffee to the intricate pour-over methods and discover the secrets to crafting the perfect espresso shot. Whether you're a seasoned barista or a coffee enthusiast looking to elevate your home brewing game, "Coffee" promises to be an indispensable companion on your journey.

But "Coffee" is more than just a technical manual; it is a celebration of the cultural tapestry that has been woven around this captivating beverage. Immerse yourself in the vibrant coffee cultures that have flourished across the globe, from the charming cafés of Europe to the bustling coffee houses of the Middle East, and the third-wave coffee shops that have taken the world by storm.

With "Coffee" and this tea tome as your trusted guides, you will embark on a comprehensive exploration of two of nature's most enchanting elixirs, each offering its own unique flavors, aromas, and traditions. Together, these volumes will elevate your appreciation for the art of mindful beverage preparation and consumption, enabling you to infuse your daily rituals with the richness of cultural diversity, the pursuit of well-being, and the pure joy of savoring every sip.

As we bid farewell, we extend our heartfelt gratitude to you, our cherished readers, for embarking on this tea-infused odyssey with us. Your curiosity, your thirst for knowledge, and your appreciation for the finer things in life have been the driving force behind this labor of love. We hope that these pages have not only quenched your thirst for understanding but have also ignited a newfound passion for the art of tea, one that will continue to enrich your life with every fragrant cup.

May the knowledge and inspiration found within these pages accompany you on your personal journey, infusing your days with the soothing aromas, rich flavors, and healing properties of tea. Embrace the ritual of mindful tea preparation and consumption, allowing each sip to transport you to realms of tranquility, cultural exploration, and holistic well-being. And remember, the world of tea – and coffee – is vast, ever-evolving, and waiting to be discovered, one mindful sip at a time.

     TEA: *The Mythical Beginnings*

Glossary Definitions

Here is an expanded glossary with more detailed descriptions of the important tea terms and people/cultures mentioned in the book:

Glossary

Amaranth – A nutritious pseudo-grain used to make herbal teas, popular in ancient Mesoamerican cultures like the Aztecs.

Anthocyanins – A subcategory of flavonoid antioxidants that give some teas like hibiscus their rich red/purple color and potential health benefits.

Apigenin – A flavonoid compound abundant in chamomile tea that acts as a mild sedative and anti-anxiety agent.

Aspalathin – A unique antioxidant found in rooibos tea that may have anti-inflammatory, anti-mutagenic and cholesterol-lowering effects.

Ayurveda – The ancient holistic Indian system of medicine and one of the world's oldest healthcare practices, incorporating use of herbal teas.

Bergamot – A citrus fruit whose aromatic oil is used to give Earl Grey tea its distinctive flavor and aroma.

Bisabolol – A anti-inflammatory, anti-irritant compound found in chamomile tea that gives it soothing properties.

Black Tea – One of the 6 major types of tea produced from the leaves of the Camellia sinensis plant, cured through an oxidation process.

Bulang – An ethnic minority group indigenous to Yunnan, China with traditional knowledge of medicinal tea plants.

Camellia sinensis – The species of evergreen shrub/tree whose processed leaves and leaf buds are used to make the 6 main types of tea.

Catechins – A type of polyphenolic antioxidant compound abundant in green tea, with EGCG being the most studied.

Chai – A hot, sweetened tea beverage originating in India and flavored/spiced with a masala mix like cinnamon, cloves, ginger, cardamom.

Chamomile – An herbaceous plant whose dried flowers are used to make a popular calming, sleep-promoting herbal tea.

Chanoyu – The centuries-old ceremonial tradition of preparing and serving matcha green tea in Japan.

Chuchuhuasi – A tree bark used by indigenous Amazonian tribes for making therapeutic teas to treat inflammation and diabetes.

Dai – One of the ethnic minority groups of Yunnan, China known for their knowledge of pu-erh and other aged teas.

EGCG (Epigallocatechin gallate) - The most abundant catechin antioxidant in green tea leaves, prized for its many potential health benefits.

Emperor Shen Nong – The legendary ruler of ancient China (circa 2700 BCE) credited with first discovering tea.

Ginger – The rhizome of the Zingiber officinale plant, used to make a spicy, warming tea with digestive and anti-inflammatory properties.

   TEA: *The Mythical Beginnings*

Gongfu cha – The traditional ceremonial process of brewing and serving Chinese teas like oolong andpu-erh.

Green Tea – One of the 6 major types of tea made exclusively from the unoxidized leaves of Camellia sinensis.

Guarani – A South American indigenous people who pioneered the drinking of yerba mate in pre-Columbian times.

Hatathli – Medicine men and ceremonial singers who play a central role in Navajo religious practices involving medicinal plants and teas.

Haida – An indigenous nation located in British Columbia, Canada who use herbal teas and forest botanicals for food and medicine.

Hibiscus sabdariffa – The botanical name for the hibiscus species whose calyces (sepals) are used to make hibiscus tea.

Holy Basil/Tulsi – An aromatic herb of the mint family used to make medicinal tea in Ayurvedic practices and Hindu rituals.

Honeybush – An herbal tea made from the oxidized leaves and stems of a shrub related to rooibos, grown in South Africa.

Ilex paraguariensis – The botanical name for the evergreen holly species whose leaves are used to make yerba mate.

Isoflavones – A category of polyphenolic compounds found in oolong, pu-erh and aged teas that may have antioxidant effects.

Jasmine – A type of tea flavored by blending green tea with jasmine flowers to impart a distinctive floral aroma.

Jinxuan – A premium cultivar of the tea plant valued for its high antioxidant levels, used to make prized Taiwanese oolongs.

Kayapo – An indigenous tribe residing in the forests of Brazil known for their use of medicinal plant teas and hallucinogens.

L-theanine – An amino acid analogue found in green and black teas that has calming, anxiety-reducing effects.

Labrador Tea – An herbal tea made from the leaves of a shrub in the rhododendron family, used by indigenous North Americans.

Lakota – A Native American tribe who historically used plants like cedar for purifying herbal "smudge" teas.

Lavender – An aromatic flowering plant in the mint family whose purple blossoms are commonly used to make calming herbal tea.

Lepcha – An ethnic community indigenous to Nepal, Bhutan and parts of West Bengal, India with knowledge of Himalayan medicinal herbs and teas.

Leren – The prized mahogany-colored tea cultivar used for making DianHong oolong and black teas from Yunnan.

Lapsang Souchong – A smoked variety of Chinese black tea with a distinctive campfire aroma from drying the leaves over pine smoke.

Maasai – A Nilotic ethnic group inhabiting Kenya and Tanzania with traditions of using medicinal herbal teas like rooibos and devil's claw.

Maté/Yerba Maté – A traditional tea-like beverage consumed in South America, made from the dried leaves of Ilex paraguariensis.

Matcha – A finely milled powder of shade-grown green tea leaves, used in the Japanese tea ceremony and to make lattes.

 TEA: *The Mythical Beginnings*

Menthol – The compounds in peppermint that give it a cooling, minty flavor and used for soothing digestive teas.

Moringa – Leaves from the moringa tree used in ayurvedic practices to make a nutrient-rich herbal tea.

Muña – An aromatic Andean mint whose leaves are used by indigenous Quechua people to make medicinal herbal tea.

Navajo Nation – A Native American territory spanning the Four Corners region with deep-rooted traditions utilizing medicinal herbs and teas.

Oolong – A traditional semi-oxidized variety of Chinese tea, with flavors ranging from floral and fruity to rich and roasted.

Pu-erh – A distinctive variety of aged and fermented dark tea originating in Yunnan Province, China.

Quechua – The indigenous ethnic group of Peru and Bolivia known for using plants like coca, chamana and muña for teas.

Rhodiola – A plant in the Sedum family used by Vikings to make an energizing adaptogenic herbal tea.

Rooibos – A naturally caffeine-free "red tea" made from the oxidized leaves of the South African rooibos bush.

Sadō – The traditional Japanese tea ceremony centered around the preparation and serving of matcha green tea powder.

Sutherlandia – A flowering plant native to Southern Africa whose leaves are used to make a medicinal tea.

Theaflavins – A group of polyphenol compounds formed during the oxidation of black tea that act as antioxidants.

Thearubigins – A group of polyphenol compounds in black tea that contribute to its rich color and body.

Tlingit – An indigenous nation of Alaska and British Columbia with traditions of harvesting devil's club to make therapeutic teas.

Traditional Chinese Medicine (TCM) - The ancient holistic system of medicine centered on restoring the yin-yang balance, which incorporates teas.

Tulsi/Holy Basil – A sacred plant in Hinduism whose leaves make a revered medicinal tea in Ayurvedic medicine.

Tuareg – A large Berber ethnic group inhabiting the Sahara region of North Africa, brewing desert teas like baobab for hydration.

White Tea – One of the 6 major tea types produced mostly from the delicate buds of Camellia sinensis plants before oxidation.

Xhosa – A cultural group whose traditional homelands are primarily in the Eastern Cape, South Africa, using herbal teas like buchu.

Yerba Maté – See Maté.

Yanomami – An indigenous Amazonian people residing between Brazil and Venezuela, using medicinal rainforest plant teas.

Yuzu – A rare East Asian citrus variety whose aromatic zest is sometimes used to flavor and scent green and oolong teas.

Human Connections:

Anna, 7th Duchess of Bedford – An English aristocrat credited with popularizing afternoon tea in the early 19th century.

  TEA: *The Mythical Beginnings*

Bhutia – An ethnic community indigenous to Bhutan, Nepal, and Sikkim Himalayas with knowledge of medicinal mountain herbs/teas.

Dai – An ethnic minority group indigenous to Yunnan Province, China and neighboring regions with tea cultural significance.

Haida – A nation indigenous to the Pacific Northwest region with traditional uses of plants like devil's club for therapeutic teas.

Emperor Shen Nong – The legendary ruler of ancient China around 2700 BCE who is credited with discovering tea.

Kayapo – An indigenous tribe of Brazil known for utilizing medicinal plant teas from the Amazon rainforest.

Lakota – A Native American tribe who historically used cedar tea for purification among other plant-based remedies.

Lepcha – An ethnic minority group indigenous to the Himalayas with extensive knowledge of the region's medicinal herbs and teas.

Maasai – A Nilotic ethnic group native to Kenya and Tanzania with traditions of using herbal teas medicinally.

Mapuche – The indigenous inhabitants of south-central Chile and southwestern Argentina, cultivators of yerba mate tea.

Navajo Nation – A Native American territory with deep-rooted ceremonial and medicinal traditions involving plants and teas.

Quechua – The indigenous peoples of the Andes who utilize plants like coca and muña to make ceremonial herbal teas.

Tlingit – An indigenous nation of the Pacific Northwest who harvest devil's club to brew therapeutic teas.

Tuareg – A large Berber ethnic group who inhabit the Sahara region and brew teas from desert plants like baobab.

Xhosa – A cultural group whose homelands are in the Eastern Cape, South Africa, practitioners of traditional herbal tea remedies.

Yanomami – An indigenous people residing in the Amazon rainforest of Brazil/Venezuela known for their plant knowledge.

9 789367 005835